Paper Clips

An Anthology of Short Stories
about Coming of Age in Australia

Yaşar Duyal

Compiling Editor

CAMBRIDGE
UNIVERSITY PRESS

CAMBRIDGE
UNIVERSITY PRESS

Shaftesbury Road, Cambridge CB2 8EA, United Kingdom

One Liberty Plaza, 20th Floor, New York, NY 10006, USA

477 Williamstown Road, Port Melbourne, VIC 3207, Australia

314–321, 3rd Floor, Plot 3, Splendor Forum, Jasola District Centre, New Delhi – 110025, India

103 Penang Road, #05–06/07, Visioncrest Commercial, Singapore 238467

Cambridge University Press is part of Cambridge University Press & Assessment,
a department of the University of Cambridge.

We share the University's mission to contribute to society through the pursuit of
education, learning and research at the highest international levels of excellence.

www.cambridge.org
Information on this title: www.cambridge.org/9781107614208

First published 2013
20 19 18 17 16 15 14 13 12 11 10 9 8 7 6 5

Cover designed by Kerry Cooke

*A catalogue record for this book is available from the National
Library of Australia at* www.nla.gov.au

ISBN   978-1-107-61420-8   Paperback

Additional resources for this publication at www.cambridge.edu.au/paperclips

To my daughter Tayla, whose teenage years will never cease inspiring

Acknowledgements

I would like to acknowledge the fantastic work and help provided by my editor, Frances Wade, and Cambridge staff Margie Dela Cruz, Amelia Fellows and Linda Kowarzik. Without them believing in this series none of the stories would be possible. Thanks also to the staff at Highvale Secondary College and all the wonderful students and their teachers from all over Australia who supported the project and took part in it. Finally, to my ever-patient wife, Serren, and our two beautiful daughters, Tayla and Tarim, for putting up with more extra work at home.

- Yaşar Duyal

I would like to thank the following schools for their contribution to the development of this book: All Saints College Bathurst, Dandenong High School, Glen Waverley Secondary College, Kalamunda Senior High School, Killester College, Kingston High School, Melbourne Grammar School, Northern Territory Open Education Centre (NTOEC), Our Lady of Mercy College, Pembroke School, Rockhampton Girls Grammar School, Sandgate District State High School, St. Aloysius College, St. Patrick's Marist College Dundas, Sydney Girls High School and Wesley College.

A special thanks to Marion Visentin and the staff at Cambridge University Press, especially Amelia Fellows, and to Pawel Zawislak for the illustrations.

To Yaşar, thank you once again for your tireless dedication, effort and enthusiasm for this project.

And, of course, to all the amazing authors who contributed to this book. Thank you for having the courage to share your stories with the world.

- Margie Dela Cruz (Publisher)

Contents

Foreword

The stories in *Paper Clips* tell us about young people's concerns, families and choices, and how these choices have a significant impact on their lives.

Learning to adapt is the key to surviving the complex teenage world of today. Jasmine Yiamkiati explains the importance of learning to love oneself, while Elizabeth Morgan tells of the crucial role environment plays when it comes to fitting in. Karyn Tee unlocks some of the myths about Australian adolescents before Ben Black urges us not to let others push us around.

Some events and people from our childhood will always have a special place in our memory. Charlotte Brew's narrator shares a traumatic childhood experience, while Rose Rosen views childhood through the lense of the 'red sculpture'. Rosie McCrossin smells 'melting bitumen and sweet after-rain' at the end of primary school and Shaun Moeller tells of a childhood liberated and inspired by surfing.

If Australia is the home of multiculturalism, Australian teenagers are its pillars. Helen Qin's individuality does not stop her from embracing her heritage, while Karen Huang pulls her migrant parents' suitcase apart to discover her own path. Ryan Harris and Elena Ng encourage us to chase our dreams with courage, whatever the circumstances.

Australian teenagers often struggle in their search for identity. Christine Eid's narrator finds her refuge at an all girls' school, while Arun Patel opens a window into the identity of a teenage boy. Fiona Lam's metaphors of 'Chinatown' and the 'Barden clock' echo the question asked by Erin Caulley: what does it mean 'to be or not to be'?

As adolescents search for their true identity, many discover love along the way. Alexander Sirian Be approaches love spiritually, while Jessica Chisholm explores the healing power of love. The final two stories on love explore familial love, with both Keeley Roberts and Milan Kantor telling of the powerful love between siblings.

Being a teenager in Australia is not for the fainthearted. Catriona Cowie explores a teenager's grief, while Amie Rovacsek writes about the willpower of a teenager coming to terms with injury. Samantha Go explores how memories can bring us back from the brink of darkness, while Hugh Offor's character learns to face his deepest fear.

Many *Paper Clips* stories explore the unique beauty of the Australian landscape. Teagan Brandis views the outback through the eyes of a native Western Australian, while Maya Simpson views the same land through the eyes of a London migrant. Mathew Hill shows another side to the traditional Aussie Christmas and Jaimee Rich celebrates her beloved sunburnt country on Australia Day.

Paper Clips is a suitcase full of stories that sing 'a reverberation of meaningful lyrics to a song we all [know] well'. I would like to congratulate all the young writers. Please stay true to your dreams and keep sharing your stories, as they change and inspire the lives of others.

- Yaşar Duyal

About the Compiling Editor

Yaşar Duyal migrated to Australia in August 1993 from the Turkish Republic of Northern Cyprus. He worked first as an education aide supporting children with learning disabilities at Springvale Primary School. Since then, he has taught Studies of Society and Education (SOSE), English, English as a Second Language (ESL) and English Literature at Westall Secondary College, Minaret College, Parkdale Secondary College, Eumemmerring Senior College and Narre Warren South P-12 College.

Yaşar is currently the Head of English and teaches English Literature and VCE English at Highvale Secondary College, Glen Waverley. Since 1994, he has also been teaching and coordinating the study of Turkish Language at the Victorian School of Languages and previously taught at Western Thrace Turkish School in Keysborough. Yaşar has also been working for the Victorian Curriculum and Assessment Authority (VCAA) as a Chief Assessor for the year 12 Turkish Language exam.

He has established an English Language Centre for international students at Parkdale Secondary College and has been an English/English as an Additional Language leader at Narre Warren South P-12 College. Yaşar has worked with many students and parents from refugee backgrounds over the years. The programs he helped set up for refugee mothers and students at Narre Warren South P-12 College were recognised with the Governor's Award for Excellence in Multicultural Education in 2009. In December 2011, he received an award for his community service in education in multicultural Victoria from the Victorian Multicultural Commission.

Yaşar is currently completing his PhD studies in Education at the University of Melbourne.

ADAPTATION

Canvas
Jasmine Yiamkiati

Australia is a diverse and multicultural country. Each and every citizen comes from a different background and each citizen's background has contributed to what is internationally known as Australia. Benefiting from the range of food, language, culture and religion that all these people have brought with them, Australia is able to flourish today as a free and unique nation. Australia with its diversity is an artwork in itself.

All teenagers develop in their own way and become increasingly attracted to the idea of independence. It doesn't matter who you are or where you live. Because of Australia's isolation, it has been hard for teenagers here to keep up with trends in other countries but now, thanks to social media and the internet, we are imitating and copying overseas developments to a point where our culture has become a part of everyone else's identity 'run-off'.

I've noticed that many teenagers around me have forgotten how their lives began and do not recognise how beautiful life is. Look at teenage life from the perspective of a young, fifteen-year-old female and remember when you, too, were one of us. You will notice that there are a few youthful, curious spirits who want to go outside the box and paint a different, larger picture of their lives.

Think of it this way. On the day you are born, you are a pure, blank piece of rugged, unframed canvas. Your parents look at you and are inspired to call this potential work of art their *masterpiece*.

They place that label in the very centre of your canvas, which stays with you forever and lets you and the world know who you are. Your parents now hold the paintbrush while your god – whoever he or she or they may be – provides the paint. You sit and watch.

Your canvas is stapled onto the family wall while you grow, learn and develop your own various shades of personality, which are reflected in the colours of your canvas. Your home is where you originate and belong. The family wall is where your parents paint their values, culture, life lessons and discipline onto and into you. Once your personality has developed, it is up to you whether or not you let the paint dry or wipe it off immediately.

Canvas

You could be the youngest, middle or eldest of a number of siblings, or an only child, but through thick and thin the canvases that fill this family wall become a gallery, in which you complement each other and form a family *masterpiece*.

You soon learn that life is full of decisions. You will choose wrong ones and you will choose right ones. When you enter school and begin to develop a social life, everything begins to change. You learn to listen and to speak; you learn what makes people smile and laugh or cry and cringe. You learn that people will always remember the bad things rather than the good and will watch your every move because *everyone*, regardless of social rank, is being watched.

Before you know it, you will want to – *need* to – become a part of the larger 'community', which is universally known as 'Society'. You will *need* to fit in.

The word 'community' has been put into quotation marks because of its irony. By definition, a community is a shared space or organisation etc. etc. But is it not also what one would define as their 'home' among strangers? The area you live in, the local shopping centre and your online blog are all communities that are meant to give you a sense of belonging.

Community was once a positive thing.

'She looks weird.' 'He is ugly.' 'That's lame.' Who decides these things? Rather, who has the *right* to decide these things? Hungry for answers, you ask your friends; you look around and the answer is the same. 'Society is like a rock. It's everywhere in different shapes, sizes and forms. Just go with it and stop thinking about it!'

'A rock?' you ask.

'Yeah, because it's, like, stable and what we can depend on, y'know?' answers an obvious member of Society.

You spend years observing and obeying Society's rules until you find that the rock has scratched visible marks on your canvas, which let everyone know that you are a part of Society.

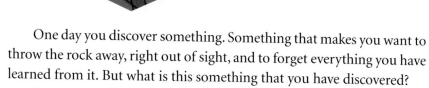

One day you discover something. Something that makes you want to throw the rock away, right out of sight, and to forget everything you have learned from it. But what is this something that you have discovered?

Society ruined the teenager; that is what. Society saw these blank canvases that had only been painted on by parents and cultural tradition and tore them. Society painted teenagers in grey, confused shades and all the canvases took on these colours. This is to be expected, since the opinions of Society are inconsistent and flawed, and contradictory in themselves. But no one figures this out until it's too late.

'How does one become a part of Society in the first place?' you muse.

'Looking the part would be a good start. We want slim, tanned, toned, fit bodies to represent us. Remember to always look good,' answers Society.

You don't know why, but it seems to make sense to look like this, although it's at your own cost, so you start to tear again the already ragged and torn canvas to fit the shape that Society deems desirable. You cut, slash and split the canvas until it is considered perfect.

You begin to notice other people doing the same thing. You find that some achieve acceptance almost effortlessly, while others – including you, perhaps – end up abusing the canvas even more till the damage is doubled or trebled. Rips occur here and there, obvious signs of your struggle, and you tape them up, yet they remain visible. Visible enough for people to question your well-being and for you to mask your pain with: 'I'm fine.'

You become one of a large group. This is the group who struggle with their physical appearance. You try everything you can think of, but it's not enough because Society changes its standards and the desired size 10 becomes a desired size 6. You are careful not to go to drastic lengths, because you have learned that there really are people out there who have to battle with depression, anorexia and bulimia. Which makes you think: is it worth it?

'Yes,' answers Society.

Canvas

Looking around, you want to fit in and so you ignore the wrongness of this. 'If I can't be skinny, I bet I could look good and develop a nice style, right?' This becomes your new mindset.

You remember the days when you'd ask your parents for spare change for some lollies and you realise that times have changed drastically. You begin to ask your parents for larger amounts of money and start to go out more in order to supply your endless need to follow the ever-changing trends – until one day your parents get sick of it and tell you to get a job.

At first it seems like a good idea to be able to make your own endless supply of money without feeling that pang of guilt as you watch your parents empty their pockets. But as work shifts and training sessions grow longer and more tedious, and with the workload you have from school, you become overwhelmed with responsibility and confused as to what your priorities are.

You start to neglect your canvas, your well-being, and become an empty physical presence, drifting in the cruel working and academic world. Little do you know – and yet you feel – how your canvas begins to droop with neglect and becomes a mess, for it wants to be free to feel life again. Your inner soul wants to live. But your 'priorities' get the better of you and you become trapped in this labyrinth that Society has put you in.

Society's cohort is none other than Love, the one thing that can kill a person while giving them life. Love is a tricky thing. As you watch your friends 'crush' on a person or become 'crushed' tenfold by the same person, you begin to wonder: 'What's so hard about loving another person?'

'Let's give you someone to love, shall we?' suggests Society in a suspiciously mocking tone.

And just like that, you end up finding someone who you wish to think of as your 'significant other', 'your other half', 'the love of your life'. You develop a crush on them. Your infatuation with this person takes over your life and you write their name a million times on your canvas with a permanent marker. Over the names of the family you already love and even your own name. Until the big day arrives and that one person reveals their feeling for you.

The thing about Love is that it can bring someone from rock bottom to sky high within a few beats of the heart. All is well until you learn that everyone is the same. Everyone is a member of Society, whether they want to be or not. How do you learn this? Because that one person whom you would die for, that one person you loved more than yourself (if love for yourself existed) – that one person you would give the world to – has left you for someone else.

Just like that, Love shows you rock bottom. Your family and friends don't know what to do as they watch you brood and wither away.

'It's just a break-up,' your friends remind you, but both physically and mentally you can't take it any more. Your canvas hangs there on the wall, ripped and torn, and you realise that writing that person's name in permanent marker wasn't your best idea. You sit and look into the mirror.

'I followed all the steps, Society. I tore myself up trying to look good. I bent over backwards to get money and achieve academically. I loved someone that I thought was 'the one' with all my being. I thought I had been accepted,' you sulk.

'You should learn to love yourself before you love another,' 'comforts' Society.

It is then that you begin to think that Society seems to have made a very sudden change for the better. That is when you recognise how flawed and contradictory the thoughts and theories of Society are.

'You don't have to be a size 6 to be beautiful. You don't have to be stylish to attract attention. You should study hard and learn as much as you can; you should –'

You pick up the 'stable' rock that Society is supposed to be and throw it, with all the force of your disbelief, anger, pain and knowledge of this lie, at the mirror in front of you and remember, from those few classes you paid attention to, something about rocks. Something that puts your friend's analogy of Society as a stable rock in a different light.

Canvas

Rocks can be melted, cooled and crystallised. Rocks can be weathered and eroded. Rocks can be compacted and have tonnes of pressure on them, but whatever happens the end result is a rock. Whatever shape, size, colour or form Society adopts, like a rock it will always exist.

You look at your physically and mentally exhausted form in the fractured mirror and see in the few remaining shreds of your canvas all that is left of you.

Large, torn, split pieces of canvas litter the floor. Your own name has been lost too, since during your time as a pawn of Society your very identity was taken over and stolen.

You look out of your window and into the sky and hope and pray that one day you may be able to grow from all this, learn to never repeat any of your past mistakes. No one in our generation truly knows what we should do or what we *can* do, but we all know that one day we hope to be able to stand in front of a beautiful work of art that is our life, covering our canvas and framed for all to see.

One day we will have *our* very own masterpiece.

Jaywalking Koalas and Other Australian Experiences

Karyn Tee

You want to know about me? Last week, a couple of kangaroos blocked traffic down at Glen Osmond Road and a koala shuffled casually over the road as I was on my way to school. My father finally won the war he had been waging against the insomniac possums, whose screeches had plagued me night and day in the lead-up to my infamous mock exams. The fear instilled by their ravenous snarls was surely the cause of my failing grade in Chemistry. It could not have been the AC/DC method used in multiple-choice questions, which is a common enough device. A boy in my year once received a Distinction in the National Chemistry Competition for using such a technique. Unfortunately, he had written his name as LOL CHEMSUX and when the names were being read out in assembly poor LOL found himself suddenly absent from the good graces of Chemistry teachers across Adelaide, despite the accolade. It was no laughing matter – I hear there are at least two regular attendees of the monthly Adelaide Chemistry Teachers' Association meetings.

What else can I tell you, I wonder? The AFL Grand Final late last month became, to nobody's surprise, yet another Melbourne–Sydney showdown. Also in the past month I used 'heaps' as a synonym for 'very' too many times to count. I don't suppose you knew the term was made popular in South Australia. It's a point of pride for me and the few others who have too few conversational skills to survive a conversation without a carefully prepared treasury of patriotic trivia. Admittedly, I am unable to vouch for the authenticity of the claim, but I see no reason to doubt it, either.

I am a very patriotic citizen. What other country has the wealth of freedom and safety that is found in Australia? What other country boasts such stunning seascapes and splendid mountain – no, not the plural, we believe in quality over quantity – as we have within walking distance? At this point, I am referring to my own city, Adelaide, and not to Australia as a whole. I have heard of two mountains in Melbourne, and I must commend Melburnians for their desire to have more of everything than anyone else, even if having two mountains quite ruins the novelty. Australia as a country is certainly a beautiful place, and we have the

added assurance down in the great southland that comes from suffering very few natural disasters. From a purely objective perspective, my island home (which also classifies as a country *and* a continent – how's that for overachieving?) is surely the best place to live ... you thought that was *Norway*? What sort of outdated ranking scheme are *you* using?

It seems I have digressed and I sincerely apologise. Just last Sunday I found myself unable to contain my emotions upon seeing the image of the Australian flag displayed proudly on a sun shield beneath a car windscreen. It is a testament to Australia's unrivalled excellence that even in the throes of rebellious adolescence I feel no desire to run from my birthplace. I trust you understand I mean no offence when I say that all other countries pale in comparison; I am simply being truthful. Sometimes, it has been said, the truth hurts.

Literally, in some cases. Pondering the definition of 'truth' in Psychology classes gives me a headache tough enough to rival the ones I get when I wake up on Saturday mornings ... because of the backlash from sleep deprivation due to dutifully completing my homework. What did you think I meant?

In any case, I assure you that patriotism as strong as mine is not uncommon among my peers, especially on Australia Day. I may not know the exact date off the top of my head, and I have the grace to admit that our national pride has been severely battered after the Ashes; but even so, we are one in this country and no matter how far or how wide I travel, I'll still call Australia home.

By the way, if you happen to work for the Australian Government at any stage, here's an idea for our citizenship tests: try to spot the references to Australian music and popular culture in my words. If you don't find at least five, you should go back to where you came from. If the government wants to test people on their knowledge of endangered Australian slang, it shouldn't have a problem with testing prospective citizens on their knowledge of possibly obscure popular culture trivia.

On a side note, must I really use the word 'teenager'? There are too many links between its use and that of unhealthy obsessions with unhealthy-looking vampires for me to comfortably describe myself as one. Nevertheless, if I'm going to show you what a *real* Australian teenager is like, I should probably quash a few rumours. I did not go to the beach yesterday. I don't go there often at all, actually. If I lived on the other side of town that would be a different story, but my being Australian does not automatically give me tanned skin and a propensity for seeking out large, dangerous bodies of water to flounder ungracefully in.

In fact, being Australian means one actually has a natural talent for sailing. Didn't you *see* our performance in the last Olympics? Where did our athletes get the gold? In *sailing*, not swimming. We've obviously been investing far more in inflatable lifejackets than in skin-tight nylon for the past four years, at least. Hooray for sails! Don't you think watching boats … do things … is simply fascinating? It's enough to get my heart pumping up to 10 bpm more than my resting heart rate, if I do some light stretches while I think about it. Of *course* I'm not merely attempting to rationalise our shameful losses. I have no idea what you're talking about.

I say, how about that word count? That's good enough, right? We should probably stop talking here. Are you sure? Why not? Honestly, what do you *want*? I'm telling you, we didn't win many medals in swimming because we weren't interested, not because China – oh, right.

No, I do not live on red desert plains. My father does not (often) wear checked shirts with faded jeans and a hat with corks on it.

Ah, I'm not saying there aren't people who do.

My year 4 teacher was one of those 'country folks'. She and her family have bonfires out in the country every month. She's been driving tractors around the farm since she was four years old. She's not the only one doing incredible things. A boy my sister once met on a plane told her he'd managed to turn his cow farm into a methane production plant. He told her he'd show her what he used the gas for if she came to visit his farm, but my sister correctly deduced that the foul odour emanating from his body was a mere sample of what she'd be faced with if she accepted his invitation.

I'm sorry, is this topic too inappropriate to mention? I fear I am not the greatest conversationalist, but I am confident this is not a uniquely

Jaywalking Koalas and Other Australian Experiences

Australian trait. My own sister is more than happy to talk to people when they request a conversation. Or when they don't, too; she's not particularly picky. All the same, I'm not sure what you wanted me to say when you asked me to describe life as an Australian teenager. Apart from the odd difference in vocabulary, I don't see much difference between me and my cousin in America, or even my host sister in Japan. We're a rather multicultural bunch after all, we Australians. You really want to know what life as an Australian teenager is like? You don't have to ask me. Just waltz up to the next teenager you see. Perhaps her name is Matilda. Ask her what her life is like. Add an accent to her response, if it needs one. Ctrl+F 'idiot' and replace with 'bogan'. If she talks about the sport she plays, replace 'soccer' with 'AFL' and 'baseball' with 'footy'. My friend has a pet kangaroo; her friend has a pet sheep. She'll be from New Zealand, if that's the case.

There is one thing, I suppose, that *is* uniquely Australian. I could tell you a story, but I'm not sure how accurately that would express the message I feel compelled to convey to any unsuspecting foreigners reading this. If ever you decide to visit Australia, there is one species of animal you must be wary of. Clinging to trees, they are dangerously averse to change and even hearing a foreign language may be enough to make their stomachs plummet … literally. Vegemite, the old Australian snack, is a good repellent. The familiar scent of the salty spread is said to calm the aggression of these ferocious creatures. What do they look like? Well. Nobody who's seen them up close has ever returned to tell the tale.

We have a name for them, though. You may hear it whispered in dark corners at the local bar, or see it in shaky letters on a grave at the cemetery. You should remember it well, just in case.

We call them drop bears.

Lost Generation
Elizabeth Morgan

SOSE, 13:55 FRIDAY

The room was stuffed with desks and chairs.

Second cousins Brad and Liz breathed lightly in the stale air as the teacher's high Indian accent rose and fell over the mixed class.

'We see the generation gap growing.' His rapid words rolled in lilting waves around the still room. 'As the technological age marches on, youth no longer relate to the environment and society as they once did. We see Indigenous youths lost, not knowing either their own heritage, or the one into which they were adopted.'

Cicadas sang outside in Darwin's heat. Liz and Brad sat, chins propped on hands, both gazing through the window at the open sky.

Dang, dang, dang, dang, dang, dang, dang.

The bell sounded, and they realised that they had missed what Mr Kundaghi had said about coloured kids not fitting in.

Oh well. Last day of school, and the others were waiting.

⋆

'Get it!' Brad yelled. He and the rest of the cousins had converged on Liz's place and borne her off with them to the local oval.

Liz ran backwards as the football fell slowly back to earth. She caught it and made a swift calculation: Jack was closest to the posts, but Daniel *was* the better player.

The oval was dry, and sweat kept the running kids cool. A build-up sky was giving way to a bank of silvery-grey clouds that had gathered beyond the tree line at the edge of the grass; thunder had rumbled through the whole day. A fresh wind moved slowly across the land, blowing Liz's hair up off her damp forehead, coming in little fits that were stronger with each puff. The group stopped for a minute to watch as the trees stirred in the late afternoon sunlight, and the smell of rain came on the storm-front.

Liz turned to Brad as he came level with her. 'First real storm of the Wet,' she grinned. He put his hands on his hips, squinting at the advancing squall. The very tops of the trees had begun to whip in the stiff breeze, even though the clouds had not yet blocked the sun.

Lost Generation

'Reckon we've got fifteen, max.' He glanced sidelong at her. 'You think we should head home?'

She gave a jerk of her head. 'Why?'

Brad shrugged and yelled to the other boys. 'We'll swap ends for a bit; youse mob can come up out of the sun.'

There was a chorus, the players mingling as they slowly drifted end-to-end. The storm came. The sky grew darker and a pall was cast over their world. The trees began to lose more leaves, blowing across the ground, stray twigs slapping against the calves and ankles of Liz and her cousins.

A few raindrops spattered down. 'It's spitting!' young Billy yelled.

'Yeah, we know!' the others yelled back. They kept playing, seeing who could get the football between the invisible posts marked out by thongs on the grass.

Liz watched the sky and land around her. Her throat contracted.

A dull drumming came to their ears, a drumming that echoed and came closer.

'Here she comes!'

And finally the curtain of rain swept over the road and across the green, swallowing the group one by one as it overtook them and smothered them in a warm, stinging, sweet mesh. Footy was forgotten as the kids slid in the mud, throwing each other to the ground in mock combat, tripping each other up until their hair was plastered with wet grass and slush. Liz caught Brad and pinned his arms behind him in an arm-lock.

'We'll have to go home now if we don't want to get in trouble,' she shouted above the noise and then stood, letting the rain drip off the end of her nose and trickle into the corners of her mouth with its metallic tang.

*

Billy followed the wallaby tracks as they led under bushes, around rocks, through scratchy undergrowth. Grasses brushed by, fastening barbed kernels to his clothing as the powdery dirt gave a little with every step.

He was alone; he thought back to last week and the footy game before his cousins had all left Darwin for the Christmas holidays. None of his other friends liked going out bush.

Living in the Northern Territory, you learn pretty quick to read the environment – if you want to be classed with the locals. Looking at the way animals move; learning to interpret their warning cries; reading the way the wind blows in front of a storm, and in the Dry its movement changes with the coming of bushfires.

Billy stopped by a stalk of small purple flowers and, after taking note of the direction its pointer indicated, he dug up the round white tuber. He followed the plant's indications and spied another. By the time he reached the creek his pocket was full; he slumped against a gum to enjoy his harvest.

Billy was a handsome boy. He didn't know it. It was his mother's gene pool that gave him the long dark lashes and tight black curls, and the sharp storm-blue eyes. He polished the dirt off his *bawitj** and nibbled the juicy root with its moist, creamy flesh.

The same charisma ran in all the family to a certain degree. Some of the cousins had Irish tempers. Liz was fair, like her father, but her skin and hair had a warm brown tone that came from no Caucasian bloodline. Brad looked like an Aboriginal boy and could fight like a champion.

Billy wished the rest of the mob were still here. Mind you, he grinned to himself, if I had a choice I would have gone travelling too.

*

Brad gazed out of the window. They had always travelled. Listening to the humming of the road passing under the wheels, watching the landscape change as the borders were crossed; towns reached, towns passed.

---

* *bawitj* (pr. bow–ich): An Indigenous term for a type of plant with edible roots and seeds, as used by the Malak-Malak and Kungarakan peoples. Also known as *pulu*.

Lost Generation

A land of drought or plenty, and living here fosters a love deeper than most for the country and the seasons – not just the conventional ones, but also the more subtle changes and the weather patterns that vary from year to year.

Brad never could understand how people around him only saw the land as dry; they said it had no life. Even some he had grown up with didn't see the beauty and variety bounded by the oceans.

Greek; Chinese; African; European: that was his gang. Territory kids were always different. It was Brad's opinion that growing up in Darwin gave you an edge when it came to fitting into the local area. He loved the differences in the bush and culture – the scrubland of the Gulf, coming up to the border; the sugar plantations of north-east Queensland; the tropical beachfronts as you moved down the coast, with each new town being slightly different from the last until you reached the sunny indulgence of the Gold and Sunshine Coasts.

It didn't take that long to drive to Tweed Heads; four days on the road, at the most. A month on the east coast was like living in a home away from home, with a simple weatherboard house rather than the cyclone-coded brick back home.

*

Liz ran up the wooden steps into the back laundry, her hair stiff with salt. The booming of the surf followed her into the lounge overlooking the beachfront.

'Can I've a cuppa tea?'

Her mother smiled at her above the rim of a teacup. 'Yes, if you want.'

'Thanks.'

She thumped into the kitchen and flicked the switch on the kettle. Tea was good on a day like this. She poured herself a steaming mug and left the bag in; her feet left wet marks on the floorboards as she joined her mother and Uncle Steve at the table. Steve grinned.

'You going out again?'

'Yup. After lunch me an' Brad are going to take the boards out.' She sipped the tea, good, strong and black after the dehydration of the salt and sun.

Coast life is good. The wind never stops blowing, and the air is less humid than in the Territory. Everything is white and fresh. The sand is white. Even the houses are white-painted weatherboard.

White foam capped the waves when she went back out to meet Brad on the beach across the road from the holiday house. The roaring of the waves was constant and people mingled further along where the lifesavers' flags were. They ran over the burning sand until they reached the water level and cooled their feet in the rippling tide. Liz strapped her surfboard's ankle-rope to her wrist; it was easier to manage that way.

'Come on!' Brad was already wading out. Liz snatched her board and splashed out with him.

The wind blew the sea into her face as she half-floated, half-hopped out to the breakers with the rhythm of the waves. She heaved herself onto the fibreglass and started to paddle. The waves were big now; she dipped into the troughs and halfway up the next face-dived under its crest, coming out spluttering and blind, hoping that the next wave was not right on its tail. The waves kept pulling at her now, so that the only real effort she needed to make was to dive through each one's core. Liz felt the next one coming, starting to drag her in. She paddled furiously with her hands, manoeuvring into position, and crouched, ready to catch it. She saw Brad do the same about a hundred metres to her left. The wave came up, up, until she was perched on the pinnacle. She hung there for a moment, and then it began its forward motion as the crest curled up and over. The two kids shot down the face of the wave, coming to their feet, boards smacking over the uneven surface as their knees bent for balance and absorption. In a few dizzying minutes, they slid up into the shallows and nimbly splashed off. They grinned at each other. Yep, coast life was good.

*

'Brad an' that coming home tomorrer, Granddad?'

'Yes, boy. But what d'you want to do with 'em? School starts next week.'

Billy wrinkled his nose. 'We can go riding, an' collect bush tucker, an' go camping.'

'You'll be starting this year, too,' reminded the old man meaningfully.

Billy pushed his lips out. 'I don't wanter. I wanter stay with you an' the rest of the mob.'

Granddad chuckled. 'You got the soil of this land running through your veins, boy, and freedom. It didn't hurt Liz none, but they said it would confuse her.'

'Who?'

'Teachers. Academic learning. Said she wouldn't be popular with whites, and wouldn't understand blacks; but you're all still true to your heritage. You want an iPod?'

'No. Why?'

'Ne'er mind, son.'

*

SOSE, 08:30 MONDAY

'Last year you focused on technological advances and their impact on society. This semester we will be studying Indigenous History.'

The clipped English voice paused as the blue eyes swept the class. 'None of you, no matter how multicultural our society, would understand the values that shaped the Australian lifestyle of yesterday's or today's generation, both on the White side and the Indigenous Dreaming.'

Brad and Liz exchanged a tired grin. They didn't fit with their peers; for they knew how to do both.

The Fight
Ben Black

At first, I didn't get it. Gordon never talked to me. No one did. Why did he invite me into the bush on Saturday? At first, I thought maybe he wanted to be mates. But now I realise how wrong I was.

I'm John. I'm fourteen and nobody ever talks to me so I just keep to myself. And that's why I was so excited. Gordon, the kid at school that everybody wanted to be friends with, invited me, the quiet, pale nerdy kid, to go for a bushwalk with him and his friends.

I arrived at the trail at noon and there they were, just waiting for me. I can't believe I didn't see it coming, with those smug smirks and snickers. Gordon seemed so pleased to see me, but not like I thought.

'Come on,' Gordon said, 'we have something to show you.'

And indeed they did.

We walked through the bush for half an hour, making awkward small talk. When we arrived at our apparent destination, I was confused. There was nothing here to show me.

But their smug expressions showed me everything I needed to see. They didn't want to be friends. They just wanted to bully me.

Before I could even signal to my body to run, Joe – Gordon's right-hand man – grabbed me from behind. I didn't even bother to struggle; he was huge.

I'd already decided I didn't like Gordon at all.

'How stupid are you?' he asked, half laughing, half dead serious. 'Did you actually think we wanted to be friends with *you*?' He kept laughing, sounding increasingly maniacal. I thought he just sounded dumb. And this made me want to laugh.

'That's just hilarious,' he finished.

I tried to hold my own and keep calm. 'Are you finished with your lame monologue?' I said coolly. 'You're boring me.' As soon as I said that I knew I was going to regret it, a lot.

Gordon's smirk faded. He didn't have a comeback and just scowled. Joe still had me.

Gordon came over and hit me in the chest, winding me. His friends laughed. I didn't see what was so funny. Gasping for air, I raised my head,

looked him in the eyes and smiled. I wasn't going to let him think he'd beaten me.

Gordon swung at my face. I ducked and his fist hit Joe's face. He let go and grasped his bloody nose.

I started running. There was no time to waste. They were shouting behind me but I didn't look back. I had to get away from these cowards. It's easy to think you're tough when you've got other people making you look tough. But try standing there on your own. Then what? And that's when it occurred to me.

I stopped running and turned around. And like I expected, they caught up and surrounded me. Gordon stood directly in front of me. His face was caught in the harsh sunlight.

'You're dead,' he said, signalling his gang to close in around me.

'You think you're tough, don't you?' I said, trying to stay calm and collected. 'Yet you only ever attack in a pack. Never alone. If you were half as tough as you think you are, you'd face me alone.'

'You think it's over? Think again. Back off, boys.'

He moved in on me and swung his fist wildly. He swung and missed, swung and missed, swung and missed. He was stronger than me, but he couldn't land a hit. My hits connected and he stumbled, over and over, but he never stayed down for long. I couldn't keep playing with him; I had to take him out.

It was a clumsy move but it worked. I swept at his leg and tripped myself up. But I brought him with me. For a brief moment arms were flailing, but then my fist hit his face. He stopped moving. I had won.

*

Some weeks have passed since the incident in the bush and now people are being a bit nicer to me at school. Gordon's previous victims are now my friends. His gang keep to themselves. I don't think they're going to bother anyone any more.

Canvas

Research and Discussion

1   According to Jasmine, teenagers 'originate and belong' at home. What does the author mean by 'Your parents now hold the paintbrush' and 'family wall'?

Do you think all teenagers are influenced and shaped as much by their family, regardless of where and when they grow up? Discuss as a class some of the ways in which our families or particular family members may have influence over us as teenagers. Use examples from the story to support your ideas.

2   The author describes society as a 'rock' and expresses her views of society. What are some of the author's views on fitting into society? Use her examples of 'appearances' and 'decisions' to support your explanations.

3   What is the lesson that society teaches us about love, according to the author? Discuss with a partner and explain in your book what she means by 'One day we will have *our* very own masterpiece' at the end of the story. Then share your answer with the whole class.

Writing and Creating

1   The author uses examples of figurative language. Metaphor is one of them. The title 'Canvas' is a metaphor for a teenager. Find and write three other examples of figurative language used in 'Canvas' including an example of personification, in which non-human objects or institutions are given human qualities.

2   As a teenager, how do you feel about your community and growing up in Australia? Write a 300-word instructional piece for a school magazine giving advice about society to other teenagers in Australia. Your title can be 'An Australian Teenager's Manual on Society'.

3   Ask a classmate, a parent and a grandparent how they feel about issues such as the family's influence, society's rules, decisions, love and the importance of appearance to see if these have changed over different generations. Report your findings to the whole class.

Jaywalking Koalas and Other Australian Experiences

Research and Discussion

1   Karyn dares the readers to 'try to spot the references to Australian music and popular culture' in her writing. Some of these include 'I'll still call Australia home', 'Matilda', 'bogan', 'Vegemite', 'drop bear' and 'Ashes'. Research and find out how each one of these relates to Australian lifestyle and culture. Find and add another two Australian cultural references that are not mentioned in the text.

2   Karyn's reflections on life as an Australian teenager display many uniquely Australian examples. However, she mentions some of these as 'rumours'. What are these 'rumours' that Karyn talks about when it comes to the stereotypical Australian teenager's image? What are some of the other stereotypes you know that are uniquely Australian?

3   A drop bear is a fictional Australian marsupial. Why do you think the author includes a warning about drop bears in the text? Is this part of her mocking tone? How many other mythical Australian animals do you know about? Find out and write about them in your book.

Writing and Creating

1   The author uses an informal narrative style where she directly involves her readers in the conversation and addresses them, mostly by asking questions. Can you find examples of sentences and questions she uses in her text that demonstrate this? Write these in your book and explain the author's purpose in using them in the text.

2   The author expresses her unwillingness to use the word 'teenager' due to unfortunate uses of the word among people in Australia. Discuss the Pluses, the Minuses and the Interesting Facts (PMI) about Australian teenagers living in Australia today. In class, work in groups of four to design a poster portraying a typical Australian teenager to other teenagers in the world. Use pictures and a specific title as part of your poster.

3   Sarcasm is defined as 'the use of irony to mock or convey contempt'. The author uses sarcasm and irony many times in the text. One example of this is her description of Australian experiences at the last Olympics. First explain her use of sarcasm in her references to the Olympics and then find and explain another example of sarcasm in the text.

Lost Generation

Research and Discussion

1   Consider whether it is easier for teenagers than adults to fit in, or for people from a different racial or ethnic background from that of the majority. Use some of the ideas about Indigenous youth mentioned in the story and discuss these in relation to their fitting in and how it is different from, or similar to, fitting in in a city, suburb or foreign country.

2   Are the characters in the story similar to you or your friends? How do you relate to the characters Brad, Liz and Billy as a teenager? What separates the two cousins and Billy?

3   The author vividly portrays the influence of the landscape and the environment on life in the story. Find examples of how the landscape reflects the thoughts and feelings about adaptation in some of the characters in the story.

Writing and Creating

1   'Lost Generation' uses strong, vivid descriptions to give the readers an intimate feeling of the land and the environment. Re-read the parts where the teenagers are playing footy and where Brad and Liz are out surfing. Note down the adjectives and words describing different senses (sight, hearing, touch, taste and smell). Now try to write a similar paragraph of four to five sentences, using at least two senses to describe the landscape or environment on your last holiday away from home.

2   The author uses examples of different accents and language styles in her story. These include an Irish accent as well as a broad Australian accent and teenage language style. What is the purpose of doing this? Work with a partner to choose two such examples from the story and rewrite these using a different accent or language style (e.g. change the teenage language style to a style used by an elderly person). Share your examples by reading them out loud to the whole class.

3   Rewrite a section of the story as a diary entry or write your own diary entry about fitting in or experiencing a landscape in the first person, using a narrator.

The Fight

Research and Discussion

1   a   When and how does the reader predict for the first time that the story is about bullying and/or that John is a victim of bullying? Explain your answer using examples from the story.

     b   How does John react to the bullies? Do you think this is the right way to respond to a bully? How would you react?

     c   Research and find statistical information about bullying in Australian schools. Discuss your findings with the rest of the class.

2   Explore the issue of bullying from both the bully's and the victim's perspectives in relation to fitting in. Use examples from the story of John and Gordon to help you.

3   List the stereotypical qualities of a bully as displayed by Gordon and his friends in 'The Fight'. Do they fit in with the qualities of a bully you know, or are they different? Compare and contrast, in a group of three or four, the differences and the similarities between the victim and the bullies in the story and other possible scenarios and characters from your experiences. Present your group's views to the rest of the class.

Writing and Creating

1   Have you ever been bullied, or known someone who has been? How was your or their reaction similar or different to John's in the story? Write about how you/they felt and how you/they resolved this issue, if it was resolved. What would you, or should they, do differently and why?

2   In pairs, come up with step-by-step suggestions on how to prevent bullying in Australian schools. Prepare a five-minute speech or PowerPoint presentation to present your results to the class. Make sure you include visual elements in your presentation.

3   Write a 500–600-word short story about bullying written from a bully's perspective. Vary your sentences and in particular make sure that your story has short sentences for describing action and creating suspense.

A Memory Blank, of the Most Awkward Kind

Charlotte Brew

Yearbooks. I hate them. We all look back to see how far we've come and marvel at our cute baby pictures. Except I can't go back. No, seriously, I can't. It's physically impossible. It's like trying to find the acceleration of a car without knowing the initial velocity. Sorry, I'm a physics nerd. But my point is that I have no memories before the age of ten. Well, except for one. But I don't want to talk about that. Not yet, anyway.

So where was I? Oh right, baby pictures and physics analogies. Now you see, what I was basically trying to say with that string of science jargon was that if you don't know where the car started from, you can't figure out how far it's travelled. And my life is as simple as that.

Simple. Ha.

So here's where my life jumps in. We all know that stuff about teenagers blossoming and growing up and becoming adults. Except that, once again, I've got nothing to grow up from. Is this getting frustrating for you? Try living in my brain (not that you'd find much). Fortunately I have a decent sense of humour, which is a necessary defence mechanism for anyone with this sort of mental issue.

So are you intrigued? Curious as to what happened to me? Well, there's nothing really (ha, get it?) except for that one big event. So how 'bout I let you in on it?

You see, when I was about seven years old I managed to get lost. Being a true Aussie kid, I lived in the middle of nowhere on a big farm. And so I wandered after some cows, a regular habit I'm told I had, and of course I got lost.

Now this shouldn't have been too much of a problem, as I knew the farm very well and could get back with ease. What I didn't realise was that one of our fences had been knocked down, and so following a herd of curious cows landed me in deep trouble. Quite literally.

I was blindly following the cows until I realised they'd changed direction to avoid walking down a hill (cows can walk uphill but can't walk downhill) and before I knew it I went tumbling down a slope. By the time I'd crawled back up, the cows were long gone and it was beginning

to get dark. I was cold. I was hungry. I was tired. And, for the first time I can remember, I felt scared.

I heard a low baying. It wasn't a cow, but it sounded like a farm animal. The farm was all I knew, and in a strange unfamiliar place it was all I wanted.

So I followed it. I didn't run, because I might scare the creature, but time was growing short. The sun was nearly gone, and I couldn't see my feet. My jeans and jacket gave me little protection from the bitingly cold wind, which managed to chill every inch of my body.

I forced myself to focus on the animal. I trudged through light undergrowth with a steady determination. My mind zoned in like a tunnel, shutting out every other light but the one at the end.

However, another sound soon caught my attention. I could hear something that was not a common farm animal. Something my instincts had been alerted to all my life. Something that could kill me.

Snake.

Ah, just great – not. Well, that's probably not the exact thought I had, but it's close enough. And of course it was not just a friendly green tree python that sits on your back porch annoying your dogs, it was a brown snake.

That reptile still scares me in my dreams. It was a mother, and I was in her territory. Snakes are big trouble anyway, but when you're seven, you're little. Like seriously little.

Nonetheless, I knew what to do: stand still, do my best not to annoy it and it would pass.

But the baying was getting fainter and I was losing the sound. I didn't have time to wait for the snake to slither on her way. And she might not go away. This looked like her home. For the second time in my life, I was scared.

I ran. What a fool, I think now, but I can't change the past. Oh, how I wish I could.

So I was running and the snake was hissing and following after me. The dark was blinding me; I bumped into several trees. I let out a scream

as I felt a branch snag my foot. I practically did a Superman off the top of a crest and fell into damp underbrush. Panting, I tried to move but pain was shooting through my hands and knees. For a moment I struggled in the leaves and debris, then my body collapsed. I turned my gaze up from the insect-ridden ground and saw a teenage girl lying dead next to me.

I would have screamed, but I didn't have the strength. I just stared at her in horror as my body shook with exhaustion.

She was beautiful. Long blonde hair, dark brown eyes and the body of a hardworking farm girl who spent her days herding stubborn sheep into trailers. She was in a red hoodie and navy-blue sports shorts. I thought she had been jogging. At the time it was all that I noticed. However, what I later recalled over the years as the memory haunted me, were the tears in her clothes. Her legs, slender with firm thigh muscles, were riddled with cuts and abrasions. Her hair was full of leaf litter, and there were three long scratches running down the side of her face. As if someone had clawed her with their bare hands. Her eyes were wide open, startlingly like Bambi's eyes when the hunter shot his mother. Ironically, that's how she had been killed: shot with a 22 in the chest as she ran. Or at least, that's what I think she had been doing.

Then of course the snake caught up. She always surprises me in my dreams, because sometimes I'm spending an eternity looking at the girl. There's something so captivating, and yet equally horrifying, about her. But at least I know at that stage that the nightmare is almost over. The snake comes skittering down the hill. In a final attempt, I manage to roll away from the monster and throw my hands up to protect my face. A sharp sting pricks my arm, followed by a terrifying burning sensation running up my veins. It ends with a cold chill. My arms fall to my sides. It doesn't take long for the dreaded paralysis to take full effect. Satisfied, the creature returns to her young.

The last thing I remember was how warm the girl felt as I drifted into unconsciousness, the stars winking at me as if this were all a big joke.

The rest of my life has been told to me by other people. I was found a few hours later by hunting dogs, though it probably wasn't my scent they were catching on to. The adults thought we were both dead, but one of the dogs stirred a response in my cold, near-lifeless form.

I was rushed to hospital and pumped full of antivenom. I went into renal failure and was put into an induced coma for seven days. When I came out of it I couldn't move. My muscles had deteriorated severely and my blood wasn't clotting properly, in spite of several blood transfusions. I'd almost gone into multiple organ failure when they tried to bring me back to consciousness after three days. It was one of the most severe cases of snakebite ever recorded.

But worse than all the physical ailments was this: when I finally woke up, I had no idea who any of the people around me were. I didn't recognise my own family.

It was as if my brain had tried to perform a complete memory wipe, like a computer. Except it had seriously failed. If I was going to lose all my memories, I might as well have lost the one that continued to wake me up screaming for years after.

I started making memories again when I was ten or eleven. I very vaguely remember watching my sister's birthday party from another room. She looked happy. They all did when I wasn't around. My parents didn't take my amnesia well. It was like bringing home a stranger instead of their child. At times I would say something that would remind them of the old me, but then I would revert back to this unknown being with a traumatic experience dictating her life. But, really, I might as well have died out in that bush. My family never got me back. My parents split up a few years later.

Eventually I was sent to boarding school. Many people hate the idea of becoming a boarder. I loved it, though. Here I wasn't numbly drifting through life trying to avoid the past. I wasn't trying to be who my parents wanted me to be. (You have no idea how heartbreaking it is to try to be 'yourself' and watch your parents' faces fall as you fail.) I could be whoever I wanted to be. Besides, I couldn't improve on the masquerade I'd been performing in. I'm ready to begin again. Or, at least, I'm going to try.

So I'm on a mission: to find out what happened and put it behind me. Oh, and to figure out just who I am. Not who I used to be – I've heard plenty about that – but rather what I shall become. I'm seventeen; it's the perfect age to grow up. Plus I have a goal: to find out what happened to that girl.

So when the school's student photographer finally tracked me down to wrestle baby pictures out of me, I handed over the one photo I had kept from my childhood: the one of my seven-year-old self lying paralysed with a hunting dog at my left and a dead girl to my right.

That ought to teach them to ask me for baby pictures.

A Memory Blank, of the Most Awkward Kind

Bajo El Sol Jaguar
Rose Rosen

The photograph showed the marks of time – the distinct haze of a picture taken in a decade when cameras were clumsy black boxes carried by eager parents making memories of their children. The same cameras can still be found today, carried by the now grown children who used to pose in front of them. The only difference is that the once state-of-the-art black boxes are now fashionable lumps of nostalgia swinging around the necks of young adults.

I have always liked looking through my mother's photograph albums. Since the arrival of the digital camera, she has converted all her memories into soft form. But I like the hard copies – their slightly sticky finish, their yellowing corners. Like people, photos of the past mature; the increasingly antique photo paper seems to gather wisdom as it projects in eternal perfect tense a moment of the past.

On this occasion I had pulled the albums out after dinner, gazing over the still-shots of our family history in an attempt to postpone looming evening chores. I stopped midway through the album when a black speck on a photo caught my eye – some dust had gathered over the evening sky of the print. I scratched the marks away, peeling with it faint streaks of the empty twilight. As my hand brushed the final bits of dust from its surface, a pair of young eyes drew my attention. They were my eyes, my young eyes that had barely counted seven Christmases, shining with unaffected glee in the fading light of the desert dusk. I was topless, my yet-to-form breasts and pale stomach sticking forward as I threw my hands into the air. By my side stood a boy not much older than myself, equally gleeful, equally topless. We stood together in the foreground, the lowering light catching on the red rocks that surrounded us and creating long shadows on the ochre earth that fell away behind. I turned the print over to reveal a scrawl of black ink: 'Pip and Kieran 1996 "Bajo El Sol Jaguar"'. It was the name of the red sculpture that stood tall behind us – a second red sun setting behind our youthful bodies. I know my mother would laugh if I told her how long ago it all seemed. For her it was only yesterday that she held me blue and screaming in her arms on a narrow bed in the old maternity ward in Broken Hill. But I know that time itself is an unfixed variable.

When I close my eyes I am back beneath the jaguar sun of my childhood – the warm coloured dusk rays filling the sky, as a cool breeze relieves the relentless heat of a long summer day. I am plummeting off Iodide Street, onto Bromide Street and down a dusty side-alley on my pushbike, watching the pink peppercorn trees pass by and my brother race ahead. I can feel the call of excitement as it builds with the speed of the bike until it becomes too much, escaping my mouth and calling the neighbourhood children to meet us by the wattle tree on the banks of the dried creek bed. We would play hide-and-seek, cops-and-robbers and sardines until a mother would appear in the distance calling her child to dinner and the others would reluctantly pick up their bikes and head home to their mothers, who were also making dinner or folding laundry, or feeding a younger sibling its first spoonful of mashed pear.

Sometimes I wish I had a memory of that first spoonful of real food that my mother coaxed into my mouth. A photograph on the following page of the album shows a bald lump sitting in a white plastic highchair, wearing a bib that bears the stains of many initiations into the pleasurable world of food. I have always been slightly confused by the emphasis that is placed on our 'first' experiences. The brown pages of the album bear several titles of a similar nature: 'Pip's First Ice-Cream', 'Pip's First Milk Tooth', 'Pip's First Day at School'. First experiences seem always to be plagued by the clumsy marks of inexperience. A caption that reads 'stubbornly snatched from Lawson' (my eldest brother) 'who was not consoled until another ice-cream was bought' accompanies the photograph of a rounder, younger version of myself clutching the softening body of a chocolate ice-cream as it melts down my tiny paw. My eyes now follow the fleeting ice-cream as it melts away down my tubby arm, which now forever rests on the frame of the photograph. The picture below is of another 'first': 'Pip's First Day at High School'. Like the image before, Kieran and I stand side by side, this time dressed fully in navy-and-white Broken Hill High uniforms. Kieran had promised me that day he would look out for me and introduce me to the children in his form. He kept his promise – he always looked out for me in high school.

Bajo El Sol Jaguar

The last photograph in the album is of the same tall sculpture, standing stark and solitary, the sun winking through the sandstone. For many it is a monument of the town I grew up in, a tribute to the red desert itself. For me it is the headstone of my childhood, an eye gazing into the frivolous days spent sucking on saltbush and looking for opals in the riverbed. Kieran and I would stand topless together underneath the jaguar sun one last time, the real sun falling behind the horizon, leaving behind the stars and an emu-egg coloured sky. This time our eyes would be filled with less glee and more trepidation. Then the millennium would come and Broken Hill would only inhabit the bottlebrush-lined streets of my memory. The lead drove us from the town. I sometimes wonder if, in my childhood, I had been infected with so much of the town's lead that it had weighed my heart down, suspended, unable to move on with me.

I find myself wanting to return, to go back to the red desert of my childhood, to know what it was like to see for the first time the flat ochre earth meet the horizon. Perhaps all that remains of the past are memories. But I know that not even the weight of lead could sink from my memory those days spent underneath the jaguar sun.

Camphor Laurel Summers
Rosie McCrossin

The end of primary school smelled of melting bitumen and sweet after-rain. There had been eight summers of clingy school uniforms under the camphor laurel, wishing for these days, which seemed to have come far too quickly. The class was a mix of half-cooked teenagers and children, mismatched and colliding with each other. The end of primary school was a strange awakening of razors, hushed whispers and bra shopping. A familiar world was collapsing under the weight of adulthood.

Clay club was established when the summer got too hot for the ladybirds on the camphor laurel tree to be collected. The supply of clay was found under a stone near the out-of-bounds area at the top of the oval; it was wet and soft and smelled of ancient rain. The stone wall under the camphor laurel became the clay club. All of that summer was spent creating tiny snakes, pots and dreams, which dried in the sultry air of the classroom, stored carefully on tissues in the under-desk trays. All that summer the clay hole was watered with precious liquid stored in water bottles, squeezed from hats, carried in lunchbox containers. The popular girls laughed from the other side of the oval, flickers of envy flashing across their eyes. Eventually everyone became bored with clay club. It only took one week for the clay hole to dry out.

Before their swimming lesson they sit on the whitewashed grand-stands, squinting at the too-blue pool. All girls. The teacher explains to them that if they have their periods she can take them out of swimming. She will put a tick next to their name. She smiles warmly as if she has just saved them from every possible embarrassment of burgeoning womanhood. Some girls giggle, others nod solemnly. In the changing room there is secrecy; towels, still patterned with the princesses and flowers of childhood, draped around as they change. Some still change openly in the corner, unaware of what is coming.

School camp comes that same summer. Many of the girls wear tight-fitting clothes, which cling to their half-developed body parts. They separate themselves from the boys but their bodies betray their age. Yet for boys and girls alike this is a foreign and strange time, though

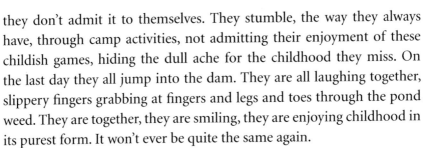

they don't admit it to themselves. They stumble, the way they always have, through camp activities, not admitting their enjoyment of these childish games, hiding the dull ache for the childhood they miss. On the last day they all jump into the dam. They are all laughing together, slippery fingers grabbing at fingers and legs and toes through the pond weed. They are together, they are smiling, they are enjoying childhood in its purest form. It won't ever be quite the same again.

At the end of that year they change the game they've always played: the game of innocent fun where you asked questions of each other and traced the answer on another person's back and they guessed whose answer it was. At the end of that year they make it something that combines their tiny knowledge of the adult world and their need to know more about it without explicitly asking each other. They run up and down the stone wall, which is still stained with clay. They giggle into the trunk of the camphor laurel, yellow and red ladybirds crawling along their faces, trying to compensate for the childhood that is disappearing. They laugh at things they don't understand and feel somehow adult, making jokes about rose petals and the school principal.

They finish primary school together. They have the graduation at night-time at the local bowls club, arranged by various mothers who buzz like moths around a light bulb watching their daughters' every move. The girls try to be adult in any way they can; they follow the conversations, dance, drink soft drink and talk. But there is something very childish about the event, about the way they feel, about the lost sandals and the way their little brothers throw lawn balls at the toads on the floodlit grass, about the way the outfits, bought from adult shops, feel like dress-ups. But they are happy and they dance on the neatly mown grass, falling and revealing flashes of childhood-pink underwear. Smiling. The night is perfect in its innocence.

By the time they finish high school not many of them remember the game rules or still have the delicate clay pots on their duchesses or can still imagine the smell of pond weed and happiness. They cannot remember the years they sat under the camphor laurel, sweaty and dirty and yet somehow more beautiful and clean than they are now. They cannot remember the summers that changed them. It isn't adulthood as they had imagined it; they had dreamed of maturity, but the difficulties maturity brought seem not to be worth the sacrifice of childhood innocence. As children they had held a hand towards the future, a hand stained with clay and grass and a love of life. They will grab for this hand far, far later in life, not understanding what they had wanted all those years ago. Not understanding why they had let the clay go dry.

Camphor Laurel Summers

In the Soup*
Shaun Moeller

I sit here out in the ocean with my mates, away from it all. The peacefulness of the ocean and its surroundings seems surreal. It's another world. The waves crashing over the water soothe me. The wind pushes up against my face, washing away my sorrows. The seaweed beds sway gently in the sea beneath me.

A wave approaches. I lunge forward and try to catch it. That feeling when you are actually riding on water is unbelievable. I stand up – there is wind in my face and I glide through the water. I can see the end of the wave and I move to make an exit. Suddenly I am pushed up and off my board. I am thrown into a barrel roll with waves crashing on my head. I make one push towards the surface of the water, only to find Jack Longbow, the class bully, sitting atop his board without a care in the world.

My friends yell, 'Why did you knock Logan off?'

'I don't care, I do what I want.' We let him be and make our way towards the shoreline. It is getting late now, so we all go our separate ways.

I get home around six, just in time for dinner. Afterwards, I hide in my bedroom and sit on my bed with my laptop on my knees. For a while I switch between YouTube and Facebook, filling the minutes until I eventually go to sleep.

*

The next morning I wake late and rush to get ready for school. I grab breakfast and kiss Mum on the cheek as I head out the door for the bus. Luckily the bus is late. After we arrive at school, my mates and I sit outside for a while until the bell rings and we head into class.

It's a boring day. By second period I am starving, watching every second of every minute, wanting to run for the door.

When the bell finally goes I rush to the canteen for a meat pie. As I'm pushing the change deep into my pocket, Jack appears in front of me. He tries to knock my lunch from my hands but I sidestep him and give

* when a surfer is in the white foam of the wave after it has broken

him a push backwards while I walk away. I arrive at my group and tell them that Jack is still on my case. The bell sends us all back to class.

It's windy after school. With our skateboards in tow we head to the local park. We're having a pretty good time, getting some really good trick lines off the local spots when these four guys come up to us. They start yelling stuff out to us, but we can't understand a word of it. They run over to us and start throwing punches. But they're big guys, so they're easy to dodge. We aren't going to try to fight back because we know they won't go down easily. We get on our boards to ride away and then I notice, in the corner of my eye, a police car with its lights on, heading our way.

The big guys flee and we tell the policeman what just happened. He calls another cop to come and pick us up and take us home just in case we run into them again. Mum's freaking out at the sight of the police car and runs out.

She comes up with a look of distress on her face. The policeman informs her about what happened and leaves. I start talking to Mum about it and she starts to freak out again, saying that they may be some hired thugs and saying how I need to be more careful. She tells me to be on the lookout from now on and I go to bed.

*

The peace doesn't last long. A siren blares in the middle of the night and I run outside to see fire trucks flying down the street. I enrolled in the local teenage firefighters program, so I have a high-temperature suit in my closet. I quickly put it on, flag down a passing fire truck and grab onto the side as it rushes to the rapidly spreading fire. We arrive about ten kilometres outside town to find a huge wall of flames stretching from one side of our view to the other. We pull the gear out and start spraying down the flames. The sound of burning trees and helicopters fills the air. We manage to clear out a small section of the flames, then return to a nearby dam to refill our water tank. We hurry back out and continue fighting the blaze.

By early morning we have stopped the flames reaching the centre of town. Unfortunately, about ten homes have been completely destroyed,

In the Soup

but luckily no one is injured. However, they have nothing left. No photos, no sentimental belongings, nothing. All that is left is their memories. This sort of gives me the courage to keep going. To fight till the end for these families who have lost everything. We arrive at the front line and start hosing it down. There are a lot more helicopters and water jets out now because it is daylight, so the fire is becoming containable. By around 10 a.m. the fire is out and we are all taken back to the Department.

We are praised and told that we will be awarded a medal of commendation and one of my seniors will receive a special medal for rescuing a family from their house, which was about to be engulfed by flames. It has been a pretty memorable day, but now comes the biggest task of all. The clean-up.

*

Every day after school I catch the bus to the outskirts of town and meet some other friends to help the families clear out their houses in the hope of finding something that they can save. In some houses we find a couple of antiques, but in others there's absolutely nothing left. We finally get to where the fire started. It's clear it was deliberately lit – it began in the middle of the night. We dig around to see if the vandal misplaced anything as he made his getaway. I am walking towards the road when I trip and land with a thump straight on my head. Wiping the dirt from my face, I spot something shiny underneath one of the large gum trees. It is a mobile phone. I turn it on and with one click of the button I am furious. It is Jack's phone.

We call the police up to the road while my mate signals them down. They take the phone and put it in an evidence bag. We are rewarded for finding the evidence, so we are pretty stoked.

The next day we arrive at school and start telling everyone in our form group about what we found at the fire. Some people are shocked to know that the reason their houses nearly got burned down was because of some petty bully. We sit down for Maths and before you know it I'm almost asleep. The bell finally goes. I take one step out the door and suddenly get tackled straight to the ground by Jack. He sits on my belly and pins my arms to the ground. He starts yelling at me about how he is going to kill me for finding his phone at the bushfire scene. I shove my hips up in the air, launching him off me. He tries to hit me with an uppercut, but I dodge it and hit him in the gut, which winds him. The principal runs out with two police officers at his side. They have come to the conclusion that Jack was the one to start the fire. They put him in handcuffs, then take him away. The school day ends, so I walk home and grab my surfboard, then head out to the amazing surf that is picking up.

*

I'm back where I started. The calming wind in my face, the crystal-clear waters under me, the break of the waves in front of me. This is peace. This is paradise.

In the Soup

A Memory Blank, of the Most Awkward Kind

Research and Discussion

1   How does the author describe her life at the start and at the end of the story? Is she happy with her choice of a baby photo? Use examples from her story to support your answers. Discuss with the person sitting next to you how you feel or how you think you would feel about life at seventeen and talk about which baby photo you would choose for your graduation and why.

2   How did the author get lost? How old was she at the time? How did the snakebite affect her health? Do you have a scary story from your childhood involving an animal, or getting lost, or discovering something serious and perhaps ending up in hospital? Describe your parents' reaction afterwards.

3   a   Describe the teenage girl lying next to the author when she was lost. What does the author think had happened to the teenage girl? What do you think? Discuss the possibilities in class.

   b   Work with a partner to research the number of lost children or teenagers in Australia each year and the common reasons why they are lost. Compare the results of your research to similar information in other countries. Report back to the class with your findings.

Writing and Creating

1   Rewrite the author's story from the dead girl's perspective. Tell her story and what happened to her. Combine her story and the author's into one 600–800-word short story (half of the original story's length). Remember that your narrator is the dead teenage girl. Ensure that you have a catchy title for your story, include strong descriptions of the characters and places, and use action verbs and short sentences to create suspense.

2   Find and bring a baby photo of yourself, or a photo of you when you were very young, to swap with a classmate. Then describe each other's photo in two paragraphs before you reveal the real story in your photo. Share your stories with the rest of the class.

3   Using words also from the story, rewrite the sentences below,
    replacing the italicised words and phrases. You can also make
    changes to other words, such as changing 'move' to 'moving' etc.
    a   'There's something so *captivating*, and yet equally *horrifying*,
        about her.'
    b   '*Panting*, I tried to move but pain was *shooting through* my
        hands and knees.'
    c   'My mind zoned in like *a tunnel, shutting out every other light
        but the one at the end*.'
    d   'Her legs, slender with firm thigh muscles, were *riddled* with
        cuts and abrasions.'
    e   'The farm was all I knew, and in a strange *unfamiliar* place it
        was all I wanted.'

Bajo El Sol Jaguar

Research and Discussion

1   What does the title mean in English and what does it refer to in the story? Research and find a photo of *Bajo El Sol Jaguar* and explain the meaning of the sculpture and where, by whom and why it was made. Explain the significance of the sculpture in the story. Use evidence from the story to support your response.

2   The protagonist in this story is telling the reader about her childhood as she goes through a photo album. Do you ever look through old albums? Who is the protagonist in 'Bajo El Sol Jaguar' and where did she grow up? Describe the place, using the information in the photos from the story.

3   What do the photos reveal about Pip's family and the relationship between her and her brothers? How do we know that the protagonist is yearning for the past? Give examples from the story to support your answer.

Writing and Creating

1   Metaphors are figurative language devices used to imply comparisons between two dissimilar things without using the words 'like', 'as' or 'seem'. Explain the meaning of the following metaphors in your book, and find two other examples of metaphor used in the story.
    a   '… a bald lump sitting in a white plastic highchair …'
    b   '… headstone of my childhood …'
    c   _____
    d   _____

2   Think of two photos that best sum up your childhood experiences and describe them in a 400-word diary entry. Include other significant childhood experiences you had, as well as your feelings about them now. Use at least three metaphors in your story to describe scenes from your childhood.

3   Use the information in the story and the descriptions of the photos to recreate Pip's childhood experiences, using comic strip software and/or other IT tools on the computer.

Camphor Laurel Summers

Research and Discussion

1   What is the main message about childhood in the story 'Camphor Laurel Summers'? Do you remember how you felt about graduating in the last year of primary school? What are the differences between now and then? Discuss as a whole class and use a mind map on the board with headings on each side for Primary School and High School so that each student can come up and write a one-line answer under each heading.

2   The author uses many symbols in her story. This is one way of creating double meanings; using and connecting literal meanings with more abstract ones in the story. What is the significance of each of the symbols listed below in the story?

    a   camphor laurel   b   school camp   c   clay club

3   The author uses a rather melancholic tone and talks as if she is a bit disappointed with adulthood at the end of the story. What are her reasons for this? Explain by providing evidence from the story. Discuss with the person next to you whether they felt the same when they started high school, or even now. What were their expectations and feelings about going to a bigger school and growing up? Share your thoughts with the rest of the class.

Writing and Creating

1   In your books:

    a   identify the figurative language techniques used in the sentences below

    b   explain the meaning of each sentence within the context of the story

        i   '… who buzz like moths around a light bulb watching their daughters' every move.'

        ii   'The night is perfect in its innocence.'

        iii   'The end of primary school smelled of melting bitumen and sweet after-rain.'

        iv   'A familiar world was collapsing with the weight of adulthood.'

    c   create three of your own figurative speech techniques and indicate where you would put them in the story.

2   You are writing a 400–500-word article for the year 7 magazine, titled 'A Primary Student's Guide to Secondary School'. Write a plan and a draft for your article. In your plan include information about FLAPS – Form, Language, Audience, Purpose and Style.

3   If you were given the opportunity to stay in year 6 all your life, would it be a disaster or a perfect life? Work in a group to design a poster communicating the advantages and disadvantages of graduating from primary school.

In the Soup

Research and Discussion

1   How does the author describe the feeling of surfing in the story? How is the title related to the story? What is the name of the main character in the story? Does he like school? Can he be considered a typical Australian teenager? Why or why not? Provide evidence from the story to support your opinion.

2   Who is Jack Longbow? Does he fit into the profile of a typical bully at school? Why or why not? How can you explain what happens to him at the end? Do you think it is inevitable? Find statistical information about school bullies. What are some of the reasons and/or factors influencing teenagers who become bullies? Present your findings to the class and discuss.

3   Why do you think Logan was interested in becoming a fireman? What characteristics does he show by travelling all the way to the outskirts of town to help others? Would you consider such a high-risk volunteer job? What could be the advantages?

Writing and Creating

1   Find and write the dictionary definitions of the following words from the story, as well as one or two synonyms for each word. How is each word used in the story?
    a   surreal   b   containable   c   engulfed   d   uppercut

2   Write two 300–400-word news articles for the local newspaper about the incident at the park and Jack Longbow's arrest. Be sure to cover all the details of the events including answers to the 'where', 'when', 'who' and 'how' questions. You might also want to include eyewitness reports.

3   Change the storyline and the events in the story without changing the characters. Your new story is to be about childhood and growing up. Add at least two similes and two metaphors in the new story.

Aussie Oddball
Helen Qin

Being a teenager in Australia is tough. Being a teenager who's a bit eccentric is even tougher. I am an oddball, with a strange sense of fashion, who doesn't swear and would happily choose a book over a wild night out.

Being an only child has given me a very sheltered life. My parents are overly protective; from the moment I was born I should've been deemed the first daughter. I should sue the movie *First Daughter* for copyright infringement. I am chauffeured directly to and from parties, there are regular phone calls to make sure I am not kidnapped and I'm told: ALWAYS LOOK BEHIND YOU!! Mum gets a panic attack every time I go out. It's always 'look two ways before crossing the street', 'no talking to strangers' and my favourite: 'Never let go of any of your belongings.' Yes, Mum, I shall be holding my phone, bag and coat while dancing with friends, no inconvenience at all. I am basically a real-life version of the first daughter, minus the bodyguards.

I shall answer the key question on everyone's minds. Yes, I am not hugely popular. But I am content not to conform, I like being an individual and I enjoy being different. I have been called mature beyond my age, and sometimes I look at my generation and think, where did we go wrong? Being a Generation Y teenager means you need to have swag. We all wear Vans, Jeffrey Campbell, Ally. It's all about crumping hard on the dance floor and slacking off at school. But I will always choose class before swag. My style is self-proclaimed British. I love the classic, elegant style of Alannah Hill or Ralph Lauren. I tend to avoid mainstream stores. I also don't listen to modern music very much. The lyrics are generally just swearing and the tune is just beats; there is no actual melody.

People will be horrified to know that I don't own an iPod. I am seriously not tech savvy. Every week people are heading off to parties, girls in skimpy dresses and guys with their pants somewhere near their ankles while I'm just at home in my sweatpants watching television, missing out on all the action and building up my muffin top. I enjoy dancing, but certainly not hip hop. I grew up learning ballet, jazz and tap and at age twelve switched to ballroom and Latin. Not very mainstream, hey? I have always dreamed of going to a nineteenth-century ball, meeting my

Mr Darcy and living happily ever after. But in today's society it's probably more likely I'll meet a young man in a club while wearing a black mini, before getting drunk and making out. And that's all right, it's socially acceptable now; but I miss the times when men were gentlemen and women were ladies. Sometimes I dream that I am Elizabeth Bennet, living back in Regency times, having my hand kissed and curtseying at gentlemen. But there would be one flaw in my plan; I am not British and I have a Chinese background.

Now don't label me as the stereotypical Asian – nerd of the class with glasses and small eyes – that's mildly offensive. But in truth, I do wear glasses, have small eyes and am reasonably smart. That isn't really helping my case, is it? People immediately make assumptions about my personality the moment they set eyes on me. I used to have people call me 'ching chong eyes', 'teacher's pet' and of course the classic 'nerd'. My favourite jibe was the one where my friend told me she didn't want to wave at me from across the street because she wasn't sure if I could see out of my eyes that far.

I've learned to embrace my heritage; I always believed being exotic was a good trait. I don't know exactly who I am and where I want to go, but I have a vision and that's all I need. I go to a school that has a large population of Asians, so I am not the odd one out. Funny thing is, in my clique I am the only Asian. So that means I am the one who's teased. It's all fun and games, I understand, but sometimes what they say does offend me. I know that nowadays 'everything is made in China'. And right away it's of 'poor quality'. Excuse me, but we do produce some high-quality products. Not everything about us is bad. I mean sure, our batteries may not even get you through the day but the Great Wall lasted for centuries! Also, my food is always on show and tell. Sometimes people look at it like it's Schrödinger's cat; they have no idea if it's edible or not until I open my lunchbox and take a bite.

But the sad thing is that my food is more interesting than my love life. Whereas 200 years ago teenagers my age would be meeting guys and getting married, now it's all about how many boyfriends you can go through in a month. We really don't take love seriously any more. 'I love you' is spoken as commonly as 'hello', and it's all about attracting the opposite sex with your epic dancing skills and smooth swearing.

Despite all of this, I do enjoy my life. I have a wonderful family and friends and I am happy. Multiculturalism is accepted in Australia and I love meeting all kinds of people. I don't care that I am strange, old-fashioned and Asian. This is who I am, the Aussie Oddball.

Aussie Oddball

Stories of Our Suitcase
Karen Huang

Families are people who carry the same luggage over different states and continents. My family came out of an immigrant's suitcase that arrived in Melbourne, Australia, in 1983. The handle of that first suitcase was dragged out of a plane and held by a single man, alone. He is my father. Every time he begins to tell his stories – and I can now almost recite the entire repertoire about my parents' harsh lifestyle, about adapting to factory labour, racial discrimination, economic hardship – it all begins with how he carried that first suitcase through a sunburnt Melbourne lane.

But tonight I, the eldest daughter in this peaceful, settled family, am pulling this suitcase apart. Inside the brown bag that hasn't been opened for years I am packing my pyjamas, sketching papers and toiletries. This is the most rebellious, impulsive act in my life. Running away? Not exactly. I am running TOWARDS. I am running towards my dream.

I can imagine my mother cooking in the kitchen downstairs, humming 'Over the Rainbow' and savouring the taste of being the goddess of her domestic domain. My father, hands behind his head, will be lying on the sofa watching *Man vs Wild*. The old man, still clinging onto his Chinese culture, learns to enjoy slices of Western life. Funny what the twenty years in Australia did to him. Anyhow, what I am about to do later will make them flip. And I am hoping they won't be as furious as I imagine.

Tonight, I will stand up to my family and tell them I want to be an architect. And that I am leaving them to study in England …

My father is a very orthodox man who adheres to conservative Chinese values. He believes 'you reap what you sow' and 'money is not everything but without money you are troubled'. Gay marriage is out of the question. Most of his conversation is peppered with references to the war with Japan, the Mao Zedong revolution or the Deng Xiaoping era. One thing that always bothers me is his traditional view of gender roles. As a child, I was always a bit of tomboy. I screamed. I had no manners. I was known to bully my younger sister. I sat with my legs uncrossed. Every time my father witnessed these unladylike antics, he delivered a never-ending I've-heard-this-a-thousand-times lecture about the gentleness required to become an acceptable 'housewife'. And

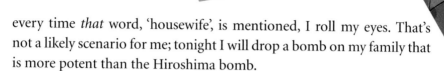

every time *that* word, 'housewife', is mentioned, I roll my eyes. That's not a likely scenario for me; tonight I will drop a bomb on my family that is more potent than the Hiroshima bomb.

'I am going to study architecture at Cambridge,' I declare, astonished at the steadiness of my voice. My suitcase handle feels sweaty as I grip it nervously.

I tell them I have been offered a scholarship at Cambridge. As they absorb my betrayal, their stunned expressions dart from shock, to disbelief, to denial.

'Archi – tect?!! Cam – bridge?' my father gasps, gobsmacked.

'Are you out of your mind?' Mother waves her spatula in the air.

'Really? Tonight?' My fifteen-year-old sister excitedly jumps up in the air.

'What do you mean? Explain yourself,' Father urges, grasping for control.

'I've always wanted to be an architect. This offer is a very rare opportunity,' I say slowly, watching his forehead fold and wrinkle into a deep frown.

Then he erupts.

'Only men do architecture! You can't go. You don't have – my – perm – mission.' He punctuates the last three words with authority.

'This is 2012. It's not eighteenth-century China. Forty per cent of architects are females. There are even female surgeons out there in the world nowadays. C'mon, Dad! Get real!'

'I said, I FOR – BID you to go. The moment you step through that door, you are no longer a Zhang!'

'You can't stop me!' I yell, heading out.

Immediately several hands grab me, shoulders and hips shove, someone yanks the handle of the suitcase. Suddenly, it flies out in mid-air and lands on the floor, items scattered everywhere.

We stand at opposite ends of the room, the suitcase between us. I can feel my sister looking at me, and Mum looking at Dad. For a terrifying moment, Dad and I lock gazes.

I quickly grab the suitcase, sweep my things off the floor, shut myself in my room. I can hear my parents' raised voices. I sit by the open suitcase, trying to hold back my tears. Venting my fury, I hit my bedroom wall with a pillow. Being a part of this family is suffocating. My father's words seem to bind me like a spell, particularly the word 'forbid'. I have the choice to disobey – but I can't. Perhaps it is the authority of a father. Perhaps it is my respect and love. Perhaps a part of me doesn't want to leave, or perhaps all of the above.

I blankly stare at the suitcase in front of me and memories flood into my mind. I remember hiding inside that brown suitcase when our family was playing hide-and-seek. I remember on my first day of camp Dad helping me carry that bag filled with clothes and toys. I remember the suitcase was full of jam, fairy bread, plates and blankets on our picnics. I remember when Mum had a car accident and we crammed it with mountains of food for her overnight stay in hospital. We have carried that suitcase everywhere. And that suitcase has always held us together.

The thought of separation from them is depressing. The dilemma is oppressive. Am I ready to fly out of my parents' nest? But my passion for design and buildings beckons me.

The next morning I am at the airport. In the end, I've decided to pursue my dream. I've left them a note on the dinner table. Ten minutes prior to departure I stand at the gate, waiting to embark. I realise they are hurt, disappointed and furious, but I hope they will come and say goodbye. Two minutes later, my phone rings.

'I'm sorry I yelled at you. I didn't want to let you go. Follow your dream, my girl,' my father says.

A smile glows on my face. I am so relieved. After all, we always forgive each other.

In my suitcase, I have my pyjamas, my sketching pad and my toiletries. This time I also carry a framed family photo. Physically we may be apart, but our suitcase will bind us.

There may be only one suitcase, but there are hundreds of stories to tell.

This Dream
Elena Ng

For a second it was silent, the silence measured in the heavy breathing and jumping heartbeats of the anticipating audience. After three heartbeats, the silence dissipated and was replaced by the delicate rhythm of the piano. The piano melody was joined by a drum, and then the spellbinding crescendo of a voice. The crowd buzzed with excitement, the events on the stage conquering and bringing together all their separate thoughts. Nothing else mattered but the spotlight on the star and the cascade of notes that caressed the ears of the audience. The singer's voice was gentle yet firm, a reverberation of meaningful lyrics to a song we all knew well. There was the subtle movement of her hands as she poured emotion into the song, telling of a love so strong, yet so fleeting. Her slow pacing against the moonlit backdrop conveyed an overwhelming sadness, as if the action made the performance complete. She pitched her voice and sang so that we could see and feel her hardships, though we might or might not have felt a love or suffering like hers. The song travelled beyond her appearance, her name and her celebrity status. It challenged the stereotype of Asians as unsuccessful singers in the Western world, and it reached out to the audience, revealing the singer's truth.

*

In the beginning, I only knew life at my grandparents' house here in Australia. It was a cosy house. Here it was possible to arrive early in the morning or leave late in the evening, unlike at my parents' house. My parents and older sister worked shifts that prevented them from looking after me during the day. My grandparents were kind to me, and as a teenager now I realise that I acquired the arts of respect, consideration and perseverance from them. Throughout my first six years I maintained my language, and found a new joy in being Asian.

At that age, being Asian meant eating rice or noodles at any time of the day because my Asian grandparents could cook it. Being Asian meant trying to help my grandmother read English recipes so she could bake cakes and all sorts of delicious sweets in the kitchen. It meant helping out with house chores, taking walks to the park and racing back before sunset ended. It meant sleeping early because my elders believed that youth was connected to the hours of sleep we had each night.

The one thing about being Asian that I most enjoyed at my grandparents' was the time after dinner and before bed – karaoke time. As a rapidly growing six-year-old who could absorb new information like a sea sponge, I learned every word to songs that I would not be able to sing, let alone read the lyrics to, now. My grandfather marvelled so much at my ability to sing in Chinese, and in considerably good tune too, that he signed me up to do a song at an Asian wedding a few months later and a man at a studio gave me some tips that would help me perform better on stage.

I do not remember much, but I do remember being excited, because at that age you didn't get stage fright. I glanced at each face in the audience and was met with the tentative smile of my grandfather. All I could do was smile back and sing the song I had rehearsed so many nights at his house.

*

The singer was breathtaking, talented and fearless. She was what we had dedicated just one night of our busy lives and a small sum of money to see, yet this was a sight and a sound to be remembered for the rest of our lives. She was a vocalist and her greatest challenge was to sing in a way that united the audience of white, yellow and black people as one. She was flawless and so brilliant that I wanted to be just like her.

*

But that was then and this is now. A year later, I moved an uncomfortable distance away from my grandparents to a suburb where I completed my primary schooling and later my high school years. After I moved away from them, life in this new suburb brainwashed me and cleared my mind of everything I had ever known about being Asian.

The thing was, I no longer wanted to flash my Asian identity because of the confronting demands of my Australian school. Suddenly, being

Asian had taken on a whole different meaning. Being Asian meant tediously babysitting my new baby sister because my parents were working day in and day out to keep food on the table for us. Being Asian meant rewarding them with nothing less than the grades of A or A+, because it compensated them for their own incomplete schooling and lack of knowledge. It meant studying laboriously for a university placement and becoming a social outcast at a white Australian dominated school.

The Australians didn't understand why I was so serious all the time. They didn't understand why I didn't spend my afternoons and weekends shopping and lolling around at mates' houses, because they were all dropping out of school to be beauticians or electricians. They didn't understand that my lack of risk-taking stemmed from discipline and obedience. But most of all, they didn't understand that I *did* understand what they said about me.

*

Beyond the performance, we could see where the singer had come from, how far she had come and where she still wanted to go. She would not stop until we understood through her song that embracing the better of two worlds and challenging one culture's expectations to belong to another will not displace you within it, but will rather heighten your sense of self.

*

It was one thing for my school peers to ignore the Australian part of my identity because I wasn't like them in mannerisms and appearance, but another to feel that I did belong in their group. For one, I was born here too. I spoke English fluently at home. I had the same interests as they did: shopping, sport, cooking, friends, wanting to make a difference to the world. But most of all, I liked to sing.

*

It had been a rough beginning for the singer, as she had been rejected many times by myriads of music companies because she was Asian. When

This Dream

she made a firm decision to pursue music after high school, her parents disowned her because she had failed to live up to their cultural expectations. For a while, she belonged nowhere – not yet as a singer, nor still as a part of her Asian family. It wasn't until the resounding success of her debut that she started to pick up the pieces and feel her parents' pride in her once again.

*

I have had this dream for many years. Some days it compelled me to sing in school choirs and class performances, some days to hum quietly; other days it made me teach myself to play an instrument or write music. I did these things in private, away from my parents, because they would never understand. With them, I learned to lock my heart away, to silence it because it didn't know what was best for me. How could it when my parents were wiser, knowing all through *my* eighteen years each lap that my heart would jog before I did?

But I realised now that it didn't mean anything to just see and follow the dream; I needed to chase it. When I see other Asians who have gone where I want to go, and dared to pursue their dreams either in the community or on national television, my body draws a deep, new breath. It fills my heart with hope, and gives my mind a fresh perspective.

Singing was one of those professions that Asian parents assigned to the non-Asian basket of careers, simply because it was only supposed to be a hobby. It was not a university-level career, like law or medicine. It automatically jeopardised the family name.

My feelings of desolation in my hollow high school years came to an abrupt end when I graduated with an ATAR score of over 90. My parents were prouder than ever, jubilant grins stretching from one side of their faces to the other. I had done it ... But as I stood on the stage, I felt torn by the prospect of making a decision that would alter their perceptions of me but would also allow my own identity to blossom. I had achieved what they wanted, so did that mean that I could now do what *I* wanted?

Would they kick me out too?

Hope sent a rush of adrenalin through me. I still had a long way left to go. As the conflict of my Asian and Australian cultures battled within me, I recalled the voice of a distant star, the amazing singer. The hush in my heart dissipated. Distinct and soft as it's always been, it was none other than my older sister's voice after her performance: *Evelyn, I know that if I could do it, you could too. If you know who you are, then you know what you can do.*

*

And I did know who I was.

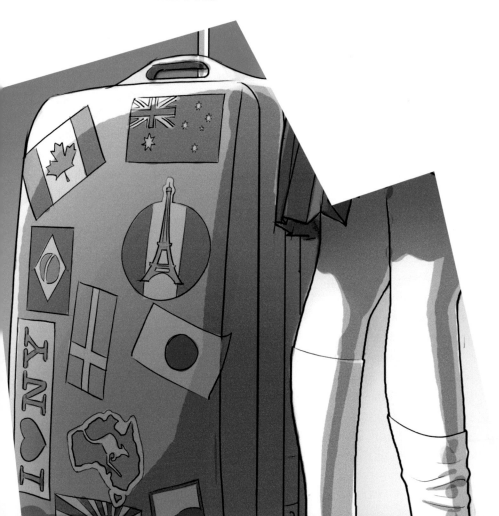

Evacuation
Ryan Harris

As the guns fired around us, we all ran to the safety of the allied bunkers. The Taliban forces were sending the last of their troops and ammo in as they slowly wound their way through the trees and buildings, pressing up on the dwindling number of Australian soldiers. All I could hear was the deafening sound of the assault rifles discharging rounds of ammunition, one after another, the slight tinging of cartridges as they showered down into a pool of empty ammo and the faint sound of voices.

'The Evac chopper is going to be here in sixty seconds; get them all ready to jump on. Let's be as quick as possible and get out of here and back home, I'm ready for a beer!' the Australian commander shouted to his men.

We were being evacuated because of serious threats to my dad and our family. Dad's one of the highest diplomatic leaders in Afghanistan. I looked across to the other side of the bunker where my family were crouched down, shielding their faces and covering their ears. I could see my little sister, Mina, screaming as my parents held her close. Then the distinctive sound of a helicopter approaching filled the air again. The assault rifles stopped. The thumping of the rotating blades got louder and the helicopter appeared over our Islamic temple and fired two rockets down into the advancing Taliban. It landed and the soldiers rushed us onto the deck of the chopper, then told us to strap in.

Too many thoughts ploughed through my head. I was leaving the remnants of my village, and everything and everyone I had ever known. What was I going to do? I had nothing; where was I going to go? What was going to happen to me, my dad and my family? I was scared. After about five minutes of flying, my exhaustion making me suddenly oblivious of the noisy blades, I fell asleep.

I was woken by my dad gently shaking me. We were being told to move across a huge road with aeroplanes parked along the sides. Here, there was another plane, smaller than the others. It had a weird red symbol on it and some of the soldiers I recognised from the bunker were already getting on. Then I noticed it. There was an enormous metal shed standing right at the end of the road. It was the biggest building I had

ever seen, even bigger than our prayer temple. We got onto the plane and before we got a chance to sit down, the engines were firing and we were rolling down the gigantic road, leaving behind the huge shed and flying up into the clouds.

Just before the ground became invisible underneath us, I looked out the tiny plane window and saw a lone figure gazing up at the plane. It was my dad. I didn't know what to say. I felt numb. My mum whispered in my ear, 'It's going to be all right, Hami; you are the protector and the defender.' I shut down and just stared at the blank seat in front of me.

I was thinking about my dad when we slowly descended through the clouds to emerge before a whole city full of tall, shiny glass windows extending as far as I could see. When we landed, all I could see were huge buildings and green grass and the families waiting for the soldiers who had saved us from the destruction in our village. Everyone was happy and no one was arguing, like when my dad and the Taliban men talked. It was different. It was my new home. Perth.

*

After walking across to one of the glossy-windowed buildings, I sat in a chair with Mina on my knee while my mum was taken into another room. I could see she was depressed and angry as a man in a suit talked to her and laid a huge bundle of papers in front of her. He gave her a blue pen, opened up the first page, nodded and Mum started to write. In the building were lots of computers, like the little one Dad had, and a small counter that had 'Café' written in big letters over the top of it.

It felt like a millennium before Mum came out, but when she did we were all escorted down a large flight of moving stairs that made me feel uneasy, out the front doors and into a car. We were driven for about twenty minutes and then I saw more huge buildings and many different-looking people in the street. They were not fighting. There was also a huge river with a small bank of white sand. We arrived at another building. It was a block of flats. I went in, still holding Mina's small, warm hand. It was huge. There were different rooms, with beds in one, toilet and shower in another

Evacuation

and a kitchen, all much bigger than anything I had back where I used to call home. I had never seen one rug all one colour, covering everything from wall to wall.

It took us a long while to adjust, but things did settle down. Mum was looking a little calmer than she had when we first arrived here and my sister was continually fascinated with the little things in our new home. After about a week had passed, Mum talked to us and said that we were going to start school soon and I would have to take care of Mina while she applied for jobs around the area. We were being sent to a public international school that was a short train ride from the hotel.

It was Sunday, and school started on Monday. In the huge bunch of papers that Mum had been handed in the office after we had landed was a list of equipment that I could see Mum had bought the day before. There were also application forms for the school, which Mum had filled in. We had bags and they were packed ready with school equipment and food. Mum had also bought uniforms for us to wear.

Monday came too quickly and before I knew it I was leaving the flat, with my sister, to travel to school by train. I had never even seen a train in my life. It was very nerve-racking leaving Mum behind. I had only spent a week in this city and now I was walking through the streets of it with my little sister. We eventually arrived at the station and caught the train to school. It took some getting used to, but we found it more easy as time went on.

The scariest thing about school was that I didn't know anyone. The teachers were strange and most of the kids were even worse. For the first few days I just sat in class doing as many of the questions as I could. I didn't know enough, but I tried. I sat with Mina the first few lunches till she found a group of girls that she could be with. Then I started to talk to people and interact with some of the kids in my class. One of the kids I mainly talked to was called Ronaldinho Peres. He was obviously a very popular kid, judging by the way he walked around the school as if he owned it. I wanted to feel like that.

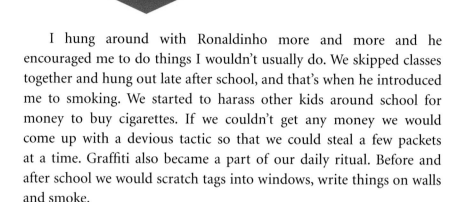

I hung around with Ronaldinho more and more and he encouraged me to do things I wouldn't usually do. We skipped classes together and hung out late after school, and that's when he introduced me to smoking. We started to harass other kids around school for money to buy cigarettes. If we couldn't get any money we would come up with a devious tactic so that we could steal a few packets at a time. Graffiti also became a part of our daily ritual. Before and after school we would scratch tags into windows, write things on walls and smoke.

One day after skipping two out of five classes, having a few smokes and drawing graffiti on the trains, I came home to find my mum in a chair at the table, tears pouring out of her eyes, crying. Mina was next to her, also crying. She had been catching an earlier train back with her friends over the past couple of weeks. I rushed up to Mum and asked what was wrong. She replied, 'Your father is back, he's hurting.'

I raced around the table and into my parents' room to find Dad lying like a statue with casts on both of his legs, a neck brace and cuts and bruises covering his face. I was horrified. I knelt beside his bed. His bloodshot eyes rolled over towards me. I asked what had happened and he explained everything.

He had stayed at the allied base camp to help take back our village. When they went back, there was a Taliban ambush waiting for them and he was captured. They were torturing him, making him pay money to the Taliban leader. He was just about to be shot when the allied reinforcements came to rescue him. He received emergency medical attention, which saved his life, but stayed at the camp for several days before coming to Perth to be with us.

As soon as he had finished his story, I realised that what I had been doing at school was exactly what my dad had been trying to stop in Afghanistan, just on a much smaller scale. I would steal things; the Taliban would take over things. They would destroy buildings and kill people; I would destroy train windows.

Evacuation

Dad went to a rehabilitation centre where he would be taken good care of. I went back to school and stayed away from Ronaldinho. Now I listen to the teachers and don't skip classes, never harass kids for money and haven't vandalised anything since. I never plan to touch a cigarette again.

I now live happily with my family in our home in Perth. We are safe. My dad is safe. I will make sure it stays that way, because I am Hami: the protector and the defender.

Aussie Oddball

Research and Discussion

1 a While some teenagers are happy to blend in or do what others do, some reject the teenage norms and generally refuse to follow the trends. Are there any risks with such attitudes? Discuss why this may be so, and where and how you see yourself as a teenager in terms of this distance between yourself and others. Explain the reasons for your answers.

   b How do we know that the author of 'Aussie Oddball' embraces her individuality and her heritage in the story? Give examples from the story to support your ideas and opinions.

2 Prejudice can be more cruel and have more serious consequences in one's life during the teenage years. What are some of the examples of prejudice Helen talks about in her story? In groups, discuss some examples of prejudice you have come across in your school or outside school. How should we approach or respond to such prejudice? How do you respond to your close friends if they are prejudiced against others?

3 Helen talks about how some current brand names have become part of the teenage image as well as other teenage trends in general. Do you think these are unique to Australian teenagers, or is it pretty much the same in other parts of the world?

Writing and Creating

1 The author says 'Sometimes I dream that I am Elizabeth Bennet, living back in Regency times, having my hand kissed and curtseying at gentlemen'. If you had the chance, where and in what time zone in history would you want to live as a teenager? Describe this dream teenage life in a 500–600-word feature article to be published in the school magazine. Include teenage issues about love, school, family, society, image, etc.

2 Write a persuasive essay of 600–800 words on whether 'schools should do more to educate young people about self-image and stereotyping'. Include a rebuttal and evidence to support each of your arguments.

Stories of Our Suitcase

Research and Discussion

1   What seems to trouble the writer of this story? Is this a common issue for teenagers? What is a generation gap? Is there a 'cultural gap' between parents from a migrant background and their teenage children? List some of the strategies families can use to 'close' the generation and/or cultural gap.

2   How do we know that there is a generation gap between the author and her parents? Provide examples from the story as evidence for your answer. Do you believe a 'generation gap' can be hereditary? In other words, if a teenager's parents' parents acted in a certain way, is it more likely that the parents will act this way with their teenager? Why or why not?

3   Do you have a special object in your family that connects you in particular ways with some of your childhood memories? Describe this object and how it came to play a significant role in your memories from childhood.

Writing and Creating

1   Every short story has different stages and the climax is the peak of the story – the most exciting stage in the story before the resolution and the end. Identify the different stages of 'Stories of Our Suitcase' and provide evidence for each stage.

2   Karen's story reminds us about the common misconception that exists among some people about females in the workforce. Research the number of females in leadership positions in jobs that have been traditionally dominated by males and present your results to the class.

3   What happens next in Karen's story? Choose one of the objects listed below (or one of your own) and one of the suggested titles to write your own short story of 600–800 words about Karen's time at Cambridge.

Objects: painting, sculpture, purple jewellery box, camera
Titles: Turning Back Time, Closing the Distance, I Will Never Forget

This Dream

Research and Discussion

1   The story 'This Dream' starts with a description of a musical performance. Who is the singer described at the start? What do we find out about her in this introduction? Does she seem happy? What do we find out about her later on in the story? Use examples from the story as evidence.

2   The author talks about the meaning of being Asian throughout different parts of the story. How does the meaning change within the story? Explain, using the information in the story. What does this change show about the author's feelings about her identity?

3   a   When the singer made a decision about her career, what was her parents' reaction? Find out how many teenagers in your class have someone in their family who followed their parents' career path.

    b   According to the author, what are the benefits of adopting and taking two cultures and two worlds to one's heart? Does the author's dream come true at the end of the story? What does she mean by 'But I realised now that it didn't mean anything to just see and follow the dream; I needed to chase it'?

Writing and Creating

1   'The Dream' has a story within a story – in other words, a parallel narrative style. The two stories come together at the end when the singer is revealed as Evelyn's older sister. Write a 300-word plan for a short story using the same parallel narrative style. Include information about what happens at different stages of your story as well as a title and detailed information about purpose, audience, style and language choices.

2   The author uses many adjectives, nouns and adverbs to describe the two main characters in the story. The adjectives include 'breathless' and 'fearless'; the nouns include 'sea sponge' and 'true identity'; and the adverbs include 'considerably' and 'laboriously'. Find other examples of adjectives, nouns and adverbs in the story and use them to make a word search or a crossword puzzle.

3   Write the following sentences in your book and identify the
     figurative language technique used in each one.
     a   'The crowd buzzed with excitement, the events on the
          stage conquering and bringing together all their separate
          thoughts.'
     b   'Nothing else mattered but the spotlight on the star and the
          cascade of notes that caressed the ears of the audience.'
     c   'As a rapidly growing six-year-old who could absorb new
          information like a sea sponge ...'
     d   'Hope sent a rush of adrenalin through me.'

Evacuation

Research and Discussion

1   Where does the story start? Who are the people being evacuated and who is evacuating them? Find out more about the conflict and the reasons for the involvement of Australian forces in this country. Also, find out who the Taliban are and what they want. Discuss whether you think Australia was right in sending troops to that country. Why or why not? Provide evidence for your opinion and arguments.

2   Where did the chopper take Hami and his family first? Why did his dad stay back? What do you think Hami's mum meant when she said, 'It's going to be all right, Hami; you are the protector and the defender', which Hami repeats at the end of the story? Explain your answers by providing detailed evidence from the story.

3   What did Hami find different in his new homeland? What were some of Hami's wrong actions and what caused him to recognise these and change for the better? Discuss the reasons why someone like Hami would be more vulnerable to peer-group pressure, and what schools could do to prevent this from happening to other newcomers.

Writing and Creating

1   Hami says 'I wanted to feel like that' when he sees Ronaldinho for the very first time at school. Have you ever felt the same urge as Hami and envied the wrong people for the wrong reasons in your school life, or do you know someone who did? Write an expository article on 'the influence of peer-pressure at school'.

2   Write about Hami and his family's lives up until the evacuation in Afghanistan. What was life like before the war? How did things start to change for them and others there? Introduce other original characters as well as places in your short story.

3   Write a 400–500-word detailed news report about the evacuation as published in a local Afghan newspaper at the time. Ensure that you provide detailed information about the what, where, when, who and how of the evacuation as well as a catchy heading with a pun.

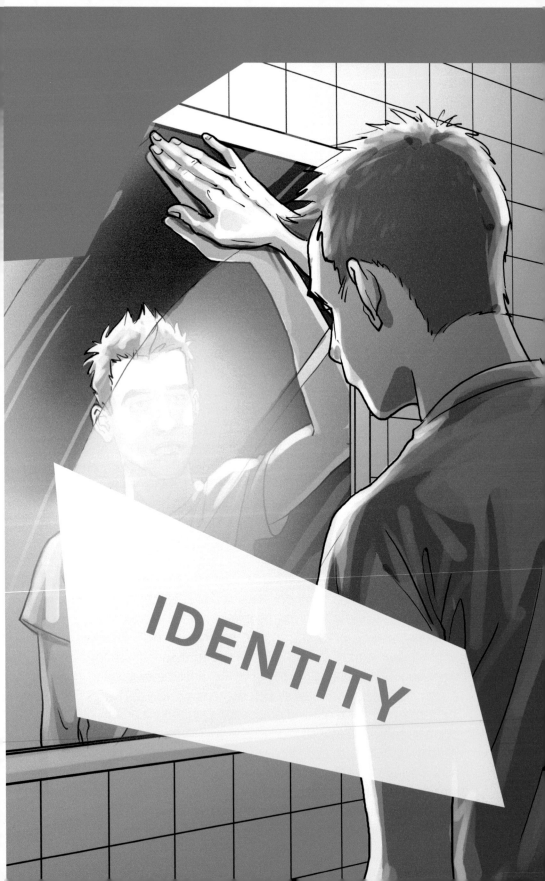

IDENTITY

Answer Me This
Christine Eid

What does it mean to be an Australian? Bam, it's out there. What can you do about it? Nothing. Because now, it's imprinted on the wall of your mind and it will stay running at the back of your mind until you have an answer. No fills and gigs, just … an … answer.

My goodness, why is the question so hard to address? I put my pen down in frustration. The question requires an answer and then a two-page essay for my history slash religion assessment. I'm exaggerating there, just a bit. Just because I happen to be a Melburnian doesn't mean I can speak on behalf of Australia. Though it is nice to know my opinion is being noticed. I look down at my page. All I've done is write the question with some elaborate decorations. I shut the notebook, knowing that's all I'm going to get done today. Instead, I pull back my hair and grab my sneakers.

I'm going for a run.

I don't know why I run. It makes me super sweaty and tired, but at the same time awake. I love the wind that races against me, splashing my body with its coolness. I never look at my feet; I stare into the sky. I let my feet pound the pavement in beats of four. I get my ponytail going in a full swish motion.

The morning streets are tranquil, with the leaves dancing in the wind and the only audible sounds are those of the crows and magpies, which echo through the boundless blue sky with the sun in full splendour. But this is Melbourne; we experience all the seasons in one day. So the evening brings teardrops of rain that we wish could quench the land's thirst on the red dusty plains in the centre of Australia.

I pound and breathe in time with the wind and the rain and reach my door just in time. *For what?* you may ask; *only time will tell*, I reply.

I find the question staring me in the face and I pick up my pen.

Thirteen. Fourteen. Fifteen. Sixteen. Seventeen. The petals of the daisy continue to fall as I count them away. Sixteen. A door that opens numerous doors, each one calling to rebellion by simply turning the knob. That's me. Another year to live. The question is, how? I have no threatening illness compelling me to make a list of the most important things to do this year. Nothing but the great unknown and that's a good reason.

The essay question has been driving me insane. I have become so observant of people and the world around me. Every morning brings a surge of people – not one of them like the person next to them – onto our nation's public transport system, which undoubtedly creates stress when trains are delayed, and excitement when the newly furbished trams are seen outside the bustling of the inner city. Public transport has been unreliable on certain occasions, giving students a late start and frustrating them in their dedication to their education. The parents would certainly be mad, but I don't think that can be said for the students. Cars flood the freeways every morning. Their drivers think they won't get stuck in the jam because they've left ten minutes earlier. But they will. All the lanes are coloured green to red and everything in between as the car's engine rumbles, wasting the two remaining litres of petrol. Melbourne has to have the worst traffic in the world. Someone prove me wrong; I'd like to see you try.

Being at an all-girls school isn't as bad as some would think. We girls can be crazy all day, every day and not embarrass ourselves because there are no guys around to judge us; only teachers telling us to settle down. We can cry and laugh freely and sing completely off key just for fun, and in ways that could possibly land us the lead male role in the school production. We dance when we're hyper and lie upon the fake grass making flower tiaras. And also complain constantly about homework. Typical, really. There are some days when I am madly passionate about it and launch into a long ramble about how it is a form of cruelty to students. And then I go through a calming phase, tricking myself into believing everything is okay. It tends to work. We are all free spirits and if we weren't, how would we get through? The important years of a girl's life are spent at high school until she leaves and realises it's been her second home.

I'm meant to remember and for some insane reason I can't put my finger on it. Oh, honestly, I really do have the memory span of a fish.

The million-dollar question is: What do you want to do? Live every day as if it's my last. But what do you want to do forever? What is a person thinking? Are you asking that sort of question of the most indecisive person to have ever set foot on this planet? Are you mad? It's a question that is meant to open our minds to the idea of growing up. How preposterous! I decided, with a few others, to fly off to Neverland or wait for the world to end. But what are the chances of those possibilities happening? How are we, a bunch of sixteen-year-old girls, meant to know what we want to do with our lives? Why can't we be five years old again and play pretend? That way we could be someone new every day. Like the postman who rides the motorbike, the doctor who gives you a lolly no matter how old you are and even the informative newsreader on Channel Seven, nightly at six.

But being the indecisive, rebellious and stubborn person I am, I want a future in architecture. Melbourne is a mixture of vintage and modern design. My friends and I have gone into the city so many times, and they often scold me for taking pictures of the decorated corners, saying I'm an embarrassment acting like a tourist, but they love me for it anyway. Every building competes to be closest to the stars in a painted background of pinks, golds and blues and the city glimmers with light as soon as the sun goes down. The Victorian houses tell stories of past events. The clashing city ignites a spark that makes us want to be outrageous, imaginative; to be the five-year-old inside ourselves.

So many questions need answers. Wait – rephrase. Many answers need to be found. Well, that's easier said than done. Where am I going to find the answer?

I'm a reader. I get so excited, depressed and crazy over a few words in a book. I get into trouble most of the time. 'Stop yelling, it's just a book.' 'Stop reading or you'll make your eyes worse.' Yep, the daily dose of lectured concern from my parents, which is disregarded in this matter because reading is a solid vocabulary and spelling enhancement. Among my friends we act as if we were seven, yelling and crying over the characters, the gripping plot and the forbidden love story. Don't be so surprised, we're girls after all.

In my mind, I run. One. Two. Three. Four. I breathe. In. Out. In. Out. The question lingers …

Tap, tap, tap …

Answer Me This

My best friend heads off to the river every summer. The river happens to be up in Ouyen, a town located in northern Victoria; a town I picture to be quite small and quiet, a place where it takes a minimum of thirty minutes to get anywhere. She returns with tales about the fun and excitement she had in the blazing sun at the sullen river. Let's not forget her grand plan to take us all on a road trip to the river, meet everybody and take shifts driving on the five-hour journey. An excellent way to toast a new beginning and a new freedom and to enjoy being eighteen, after stressing to ace a score that determines our futures. But I'm not going to go. I don't want my parents to suffer pain or worry if I can help it.

You see, it happened to them once and they haven't been the same since. Two years ago my brother was alive. He was nineteen, tall with auburn hair, his father's eyes and a smile that could almost speak. Tristan was ambitious, daring, smart, funny and already in his second year of university studying engineering and holding a part-time job in the Australian Defence Force. He went overseas with his uni class to do an innocent study of buildings. They were in the city the day the citizens protested. The protest became a riot and the riot became an explosion. The explosion went off before anyone could make sense of what was happening. It destroyed the city, the homes and the harmless buildings my brother was studying. The event was caught on tape. Filmed by Tristan's film-fanatic friend and aired that evening. His smile was the last thing I saw before the world erupted into chaos. Mum ran outside; a split second later Father went after her. They both fell to the ground, her screams pierced the night sky and his sobs shook the earth. I'll be haunted forever by the sound. What's worse, my seven-year-old brother Ben, innocent and naive, heard his mother scream. I lost a vital piece of me that day. It took my parents two years to conjure a ghost of a smile. I need to carry a piece of the world on my shoulders just for a while. I don't want to be selfish and ask for things for my own pleasure. 'I'll get my chance to do what I want for myself and no one else,' my brother told me a million times. A legacy that is mine to follow.

… I stop tapping and start scribbling. It's not much, but every little thing counts.

I need a job. Why not? To become independent is a glorious thing. It teaches you organisation, management, responsibility and saving. I need to toughen up and get over being shy because I need a substantial source of income. I imagine it's hard for managers to resist my classy, versatile charm and impeccable punctuality. I know you can't be picky about where you would like to work, but wouldn't it be amazing to work in a classy restaurant with a free ticket to all the food! Not just to eat; just to be allowed to observe would be an honour. Melbourne would have to be famous for its diversity of food. The Italian pizza, fish by the sea, Chinese noodles in those cute boxes and Belgian ice-cream – what can I say? Why work there when I can dine there, after I own my own Mini Cooper? But first, I need to pass the learner's test and failing is not an option, since I very much want to drive. It's not even funny.

One more circuit of the block then I'll get back to my desk. My feet pound the pavement, my chest is heaving for air, my forehead is slick with sweat but I keep going. I desperately need a pen in my hand before the idea slips away like soap through my fingers, which could happen at any … unexpected … moment.

I burst through the door, wrestle with my papers and plonk into the chair and the pen moves swift and sure across the page.

I am sixteen. I am an Australian. Australia is a beautiful place. It's safe and secure and full of wondrous people who have not entered your life, let alone mine. I can ramble on about things that I don't yet understand, but they aren't what I'm addressing. To be an Australian means you will be the change you want to see. The country we live in is diverse and accepting, with complete opposites living under one sun. Here you can be yourself and stand for what you think is right. Harmony and clarity are what make us stronger as people and as a nation. Being an Australian doesn't depend on your race, background or colour. It is having respect for yourself and those around you. Dream, laugh, accept responsibility, take the opportunity, cry, for this land offers it for you to take; and you give back by taking action for the better. I am Australian and who we will become together depends on me as much as on you.

Answer Me This

Deviate
Fiona Lam

Each second that passes brings me closer to who I will be. Who I will grow into ten, fifteen, twenty years from now. When my parents migrated to Australia, they dreamed of infinite promises for the future, but such liberation can be paradoxically restrictive. Snapshots of my future whirl through my mind and such incongruous associations that bombard my subconscious eventually take form in a vision.

It is midday in the heart of Chinatown. A picturesque moment: tourists with silver cameras hanging off their necks, businessmen with slicked-back hair and single-breasted suits and gaggles of senior school students sneaking off to grab a quick lunch. Of these people, who will I develop into in the future? I could be the middle-aged woman with blonde hair cropped to her jaw and sunglasses concealing half her face, juggling a cappuccino in one hand and a baby in her other arm. Or the man in a poorly-fitted charcoal suit carrying a book on Taoist philosophy, peering wistfully at the sign advertising inexpensive xiaolongbao (steamed bun) while his acquaintance expresses an impulsive desire for shark fin soup. Perhaps I'm the schoolgirl on the outskirts of the groups of friends, desperately trying to weave into the conversation about whether or not there's enough time to fit in a round of karaoke before heading back to class. From my young age I can grow into anything. Here in Australia there are innumerable possibilities, situations that I can develop and immerse myself in. Thoughts of this evoke a sense of apprehension and uncertainty that plagues my teenage years.

This is a time capsule of China in the heart of a city surrounded by Western cuisine and fashion. Various eras intertwine: the area is filled with miniature replicas of the Bell Tower of Xi'an; numerous Chinese guardian lion statues; music stores displaying posters of the latest pop sensations; blasting speedy auto-tuned Mandarin and restaurants that claim to serve authentic yum cha but nevertheless have steak on the menu. Time evolves here; it deviates, encompassing China's past and present in Australia. Chinatown itself changes, but the same types of people pass through it each day. Lao Tzu's notion that 'life is a series of natural and spontaneous changes' reverberates here. So when I grow up in such a milieu, it's to be expected that a part of me will be distorted, clouded or changed on my journey to maturity.

There's a man walking in the middle of the closed-off street, wearing a jade-coloured parka and a white beanie and carrying a tote bag filled with bitter melons and newspapers. I only know the contents of the bag because he collapses to the ground, the bitter melons rolling down the street and into the gutter. Several people extract themselves from the midday lunchtime rush and encircle him. There is a chorus of 'Are you okay?' An ambulance is called.

'At 12:15 p.m., a man has collapsed in front of … Chen's Cream Puff Palace.'

A woman in a navy hoodie cradles her phone to her ear. She takes the hoodie off and gives it to her friend to place under the man's head.

'No, I don't think so, his head didn't hit the pavement. He landed on his back.'

Reality is now stretched out. Tributaries to the river of people form and the crowd enclosing the man expands.

The words of a gentleman of ancient China whisper through the wind: 'with virtue and quietness one may conquer the world'; wisdom that has been transplanted to modern-day Australia.

Hushed, muffled words replace the previous chatter as the lights of the surrounding neon signs dim, the roar of the cars passing down the main road at the end of Chinatown quieten, and like a wind-up music box the world stumbles on its last note and a stillness falls that is almost tranquil.

'In the middle of Dixon Street. Okay, thank you.'

The woman shuts her phone and she too joins us in silence. Who will I be among these people? It was difficult to know before, but now in this crowd, I'm almost indistinguishable.

Maybe I'll grow into the injured man on the ground. My eyes roll to the back of my head. I will myself to stand (Get up, get up, off the floor! You have an appointment at half past twelve!) and my knees should bend and my feet should find a footing on the ground, but nevertheless my

Deviate

legs stay straight and rigid as wooden chopsticks. The faces of the orbit of people around me mesh together and I cannot make out a clear mouth, nose or pair of eyes, as all I can see is a watercolour painting of the world, with the colours running together and no defined lines and nothing to me is clear. Who are these people? And more importantly, who will I be?

*

Meanwhile, two blocks away from Chinatown is Harold's Clock Company. The store specialises in grandfather clocks from Linden to Pindari to Bennelong. Out of the customers and workers in the store, who am I among these people? Perhaps after high school I'll end up as the assistant, wearing a black short-sleeved button-down company shirt, whose job it is to wind up the clocks when time begins to slow down. Most of the clocks are no trouble at all, but there is this one Barden clock sitting in the corner that complicates my ostensibly simple job. With this particular clock, time is erratic and without warning either speeds up, surpassing the performance of the other clocks, or slows down, barely dragging its minute hand.

Now, at 12:20 p.m., the Barden clock reads 12:00.

'Not again,' I groan.

My hands reach out to open the front of the clock, meticulously adjusting the bob on the pendulum rod. I produce the crank from the pocket of my slacks and insert it into the crank holes on the dial, turning it anti-clockwise. I make it a habit to keep the crank in my pocket, for regulating time on the Barden clock is a daily, even bi-daily chore integrated into my shift. There is no worry about losing it (not that I ever would) because during the several months that I've been here, not once has anyone shown interest in a clock where time shakes and shifts more often than it remains constant. A Chinese philosopher once said, 'It does not matter how slowly you go as long as you do not stop.' I tell myself that sometimes because, while the Barden clock's time never flows with that of the other clocks, it still keeps going at its own pace. Maybe one day it'll find its purpose and, hopefully, so will I.

Shutting the front cabinet, I return to the main desk of the store. What should I have for lunch? Maybe some steamed buns. As I ponder over this, I am unaware of the man lying on the ground in front of Chen's Cream Puff Palace, the crowd of people who surround him and also the Barden clock in the corner of Harold's Clock Company speeding up and up and up as its time jerks forward.

*

As if by the shrill of an alarm clock, we are woken from our daze and set into motion by the bellow of a security guard.

'Back away, back away. Give him some air!'

Everything resumes as it was before the accident. Across in the window of Dee's Lucky Noodles a neglected pot boils over, its lid rattling as the won ton soup spills out, extinguishing the stove flame and running into the street, washing up the crowds of people, creating an interruption before they resume their regular flow. The man in a poorly-fitted charcoal suit finally decides on buying a steamed bun and while he waits for it he flicks to a page in his book, which says, 'Nothing is softer or more flexible than water, yet nothing can resist it.'

The bustle of lunchtime fades back into Chinatown as the crowd around the fallen man evaporates and the river of people down the street continues to flow. And who am I among these people? You must be tired of hearing that question, as I am tired of trying to answer it with 'maybe …' or 'perhaps …'. There is no correct solution to this problem. I am not a tourist with a camera, a man in a poorly-fitted suit with an interest in Taoism, a schoolgirl, a fallen man with a bag full of bitter melons, a woman in a navy hoodie, an assistant in a clock shop or a security guard dispersing a crowd. These titles do not define or restrict me in this reality, where time is like the river of people in Chinatown, Australia, speeding up to catch a quick lunch, slowing down take a picture or stepping aside to help an injured man.

I slip out of Chinatown and hurry down George Street. As I walk, Spanish and Italian restaurants trickle past me and the ambience of China

Deviate

dissolves, leaving nothing but a faint memory, as if it had never existed. The previous hum of discussions about food and karaoke, speedy auto-tuned Mandarin music and the awkward fumbling of tourists wrapping their tongues around the names of Chinese restaurants drifts away in the wind and is replaced by the chatter of office workers. I begin to sprint; the shops beside me fuse together like droplets of ink in water. I can barely distinguish between Japanese Star Udon, Helen's Fashion Hideaway and Harold's Clock Company as I fade into the current of people and, in turn, everything around me begins to interlace and an ambulance streaks past. It is 1 p.m. on the Barden clock and this is who I am, ever changing, ever flowing and never constant.

From my life in Australia, I have come to understand one thing: the reality of the copious opportunities presented to youths today. I have grown up with the ever-present notion that I have the capability to become whoever I want to be – something that previous generations did not have. It is during adolescence that the magnitude of such autonomy is realised. Out of my vision, I think I will possess the closest resemblance to the old man who could not rise up again. Such prophecies gnaw at me during my teenage years. The arbitrary nature of my existence, derived from growing up in Australia, is often a destabilising sensation, leaving me at a standstill with nothing but vertiginous thoughts as I fail to keep up with the changes around me and the changes in myself, which create possibilities in the near future.

To Be or Not to Be
Erin Caulley

Let me just begin by saying that I am not writing this story of my own free will, and as such I will channel as much sarcasm into it as possible. My English teacher thought that writing about 'what it means to be a teenager in Australia' will somehow not only force us (and yes, I'm using 'us' to show the solidarity of all the annoyed students in my class) into doing our assignments for once, but will also help us identify who we are as individuals in the sea of faces that is our country. I kid you not, he did actually use those words. Now it's not my idea of fun but then, as my English teacher loves to remind me, when I become a teacher I may dictate what lesson we do and don't do.

Sounds like a piece of cake, right? Well, you'd be wrong, because not only must we divulge our inner thoughts but we must also tie our ideas or themes into a motto or quote, hence my epic title: 'To Be or Not to Be'. Everyone has heard of Hamlet and his famous soliloquy, but have you ever bothered to look beyond the words and find their meaning? What is Hamlet saying to us and how, without our even knowing, has this soliloquy come to represent not just teenagers in Australia but teenagers everywhere?

We are born and we die; those are basically the two defining features of being human. I mean, of course, I've skipped all the inane living that we do in between, but to the average person that's not the important part. What person can truly say at the end of their life that they have lived without regret and done something truly amazing and inspiring, blah blah blah? No one does that and you want to know why? It's because there aren't that many opportunities to be amazing or courageous or some shining beacon of hope, not in life or in small country towns like the one in which I live. Let me introduce you to the wonderful metropolis of Elsinor, and when I said 'metropolis' I lied. Elsinor is a tiny town in the middle of Western Queensland, aka nowhere, population of a grand staggering 200 people, most of whom live on properties because being in the middle of nowhere just wasn't isolated enough for some. This is the small town where I live, but not where I grew up.

You may be reading this now, asking yourself: What is up with the attitude? Well, I wasn't always this way. In fact I used to be a fairly kind and caring person; I was just a normal kid, but just like everything that our harsh and uniquely Australian environment touches I had to become tough or wither and die like some delicate flower. My name is Nicole Holmes and this is my amazingly un-extraordinary tale of what being a teenager in Australia is like.

Growing up, all you want is to be like all those shiny and beautiful teenagers that you see in the movies. They're wonderfully fabulous and of course American, and for a young girl their nationality doesn't factor into your ambitions because you are so determined to be exactly the same as them, if not better. Then you hit that much-anticipated age of thirteen and realise, firstly, that you are not American and your vocabulary can consist of more than the word 'like', and, secondly, that the movies not only deceived you but outright lied to you. Being a teenager is not what I would describe as fun; in fact, sometimes it is just downright painful. But of course you won't believe your parents' sage advice and warnings about this; oh no, you have to learn it the hard way. That's when you just have to grin and bear your teenage years, which will be both the best and the worst times of your life.

That's when what I have dubbed the 'To be or not to be' syndrome sets in because, let's face it, that is the question; you have an infinite amount of choices and in spectacular Hamlet style you are nothing if not indecisive. 'To be or not to be' is not just a question asking whether we should live or die, but also a question as to whether our existences and the choices that we are making are validated or not. This question is the one thing that has perfectly encapsulated what it means to be a teenager, from all the small nitty-gritty things to those choices that are life-defining.

For some people, however, the choices aren't all that simple and I happen to be one of those unlucky few. The home that I grew up in looked normal on the surface – nice house … check; both parents … check; loving and safe environment … can I call a friend on that one? My mother was one of those women who were perfectly lovely and sociable around others, the life of the party, always volunteering to help with school functions and camps, while still having time to keep a clean house and have dinner cooked by a reasonable hour each night. My father was the typical working-class man with more callused skin than there was smooth, always fixing some thing or other that had broken around the place and, if awake, always working. Sounds great; had the whole package, right? Think again. On the surface things were great, but you can't live on the surface, much as you may try to.

My home was neither safe nor happy but I learned to adapt, to survive, and never to talk about what went on because then it meant what was happening was real, and reality hurt. My reality consisted of a mother who was not happy with even a tiny part of her life and was determined to climb and claw her way to the top of the social hierarchy using whatever means were necessary, which usually for me meant actual physical pain because everything was my fault. Don't ask me how, but it was. The fact that everything was my fault was the one unquestionable truth I had both in my parents' eyes and in mine. My father found solace from the reality of his unhappy marriage and the pain of his daughter in the only two ways that he had: through his work or through the sort of deep contemplation that can be found only at the very bottom of the bottle. It wasn't fun, but there were times when life would be great for a few weeks, where you knew the fall was coming but until it did you were determined to suck up every happy moment. But despite all this, I never breathed a word of what went on because that was the choice that I had and I didn't want anyone to know my truth because the lie was far kinder.

However, this choice of mine to say nothing and keep on going was taken from me. Somewhere along the line someone saw something and I was taken from the only home I had ever known. They apparently didn't suffer from the indecision that is the identifying mark of any teenager. I was put in the care of my grandparents, who in my world were near-mythical creatures. I'd never met them before, my only contact with them having been the Christmas card sent each year with a tin of biscuits for my parents and twenty dollars for me that I was sure to never see.

So what does growing up as a teenager in Australia mean to me? For me, growing up as a teenager means that you have no control over what happens to you unless you fight for it. Every day you are fighting battles on so many fronts that you've forgotten what you're actually fighting for. It means that you have to mirror your environment and be deceptively beautiful and calm on the surface but capable of surviving anything. This doesn't have to be a bad thing, because it shapes you into who you are; it gives you that fighting nature and determination that is intrinsically Australian. But it does mean that your teenage life is one giant question: To be or not to be?

The quote 'To be or not to be' is more than just my life in one whole question. The play *Hamlet* is my story, my life. I am Hamlet in that I have had everything I loved stripped from me, so I'm in need of revenge and incapable of making a decision either way about what I want to do. My grandparents are my Horatio, looking out for me and being loyal to a fault when the two people who should have loved and cared for me have betrayed me in the worst way possible. My best friend Michael is Ophelia, going crazy with the way that the people he loves have betrayed and hurt him because he loves differently and is judged because he loves boys the way society thinks he should love girls. And of course you can't forget Claudius, or my version of him, my wonderful Drama teacher whose love interest also happens to be his third cousin, which is so not right even though he has adamantly stressed that they are only related by the most infinitesimal of margins … related is still related, Mr Jones! All the world's a stage and we are but merely players.

Being a teenager is the best and worst thing that can happen to you because you're stuck on the cusp of doing something amazing and yet still stuck with the ever-present companion: indecision, the indecision that determines when you stop being just a teenager and start being an adult.

So to be or not to be, that is the question. Well, here's the answer: just be! Cut away all the rubbish and be scared, nervous, happy, sad and angry. Stop trying to sort out one way or another what you're going to do or what you want or how you feel; stop simply existing and just be!

Wandering
Arun Patel

'Paul Kelly?' I thought as I switched on my smartphone.

'Nah … Jack Johnson? Don't feel like it. AC/DC? Hmmm, maybe. Yeah, right.'

I turned on 'Back in Black' and waited in the freezing cold for my tram. I'd forgotten my jumper at school. At least that's where I thought it was. Tapping on the window, I checked off my homework: English, done. Maths, done. Humanities, done. It was all done. I was free to play music as I pleased. My mind wandered. As the tram clunked along I was thinking about Obama's acceptance speech, which Mum made me watch yesterday. It was a pretty good speech I thought, and I wished I could speak in public like that. That people listened to me like that.

My mind kept wandering. I realised I'd forgotten to do my Chinese homework and I cursed under my breath and quickly rummaged through my bag. Nothing. It was in my locker along with my jumper. I would have to do it before Chinese in period one in homeroom. In prep I had almost no homework. At some time in the future I think I will look back at year 7 and realise the homework wasn't so bad. Probably when I'm in year 12. Everything will be different then.

That was a depressing thought. I turned the volume higher and pressed my face to the window. The cars moved past; the buildings rose high. Some of the older Victorian buildings caught my eye.

*

The next day I stayed back at recess. Detention. It was my Chinese homework's fault. My teacher didn't want to hear what I had to say when I said I planned to do it in homeroom. This wasn't good enough.

After school my friends asked me to go to the café with them. I texted Mum, 'Can I go have chips with my friends?' She texted back, 'Yes, but don't eat too much, we're having dinner soon. xx'. I replied, 'k'.

My mum is pretty good at letting me go out with friends. But my pockets are empty so my friends paid for me. I'll pay them tomorrow. Coke from the supermarket and then to the café for chips. As we waited for our order to come we competed to see who could eat the spiciest sauce. Dad's Indian, so I did well. We eat curries, which can be much spicier than the sauce.

Going home I sat with a couple of year 8s I'd made friends with on the tram. We talked about some new games and when I got home late I felt pretty cool.

'How was your day?' Mum asked.

'Good. Dad gone on his locum?' I said. Dad sometimes goes to another place to work for a little while – three days a week for five weeks.

'Yes he has. What did you do?'

'Stuff.'

'What stuff?'

I ran through my day and then left to watch TV. At six o'clock I started my homework. Sometimes I get stuck and just stare out the window. I don't like asking for help; I try to figure things out for myself. I look out the window and think about the sky, about Venus or the Moon, their dimensions, the temperature and other scientific things. Dad always says I have a scientific brain. I love documentaries, maths theories (especially $E = mc^2$), memorising facts. But I especially love history and engineering. When I grow up I want to engineer bridges. But that will have to wait. For now, I have to do this homework.

*

The next day at school I didn't have detention. It was junk food day. Mum gives me money and I buy what I want. In P.E. we had the Beep Test, to test endurance. Most of the class groans at the thought of it, but I love it. I think I'm a pretty good runner. I usually make it to 10.2, which is pretty good.

At lunch I hung out with my friends near the locker area where we talk, stress about homework and generally muck around and have fun. Another friend played games on his school laptop with some other computer-crazed guys. When the bell rang it was fifth period, Music, which I don't like.

My mind wandered. I was talking to someone and when the teacher asked me what she just said, I didn't know. But neither did anyone else. The teacher thought that was a good reason to keep us all back late.

That night I couldn't sleep. The night light came in through a crack in the curtain and I saw my globe. I spun it with my eyes closed. When I opened my eyes, I saw my finger had landed on Spain. I went back to bed thinking of Spain and fell asleep quickly.

*

A friend texted me on Saturday to ask if I wanted to see a movie with the rest of our group. Mum said I could and I met them outside the cinema. We bought our tickets and more junk food than we could eat. The movie was good. After, we went to a games store to look for a new game. One of my friends accidentally knocked over a stack of games and we all ran out laughing. We kept laughing when my friend had to help restack the games.

On Sunday I spent some time studying algebra for a Maths exam. A primary school friend texted me and asked if I wanted to come over. Mum said I could once I finished my revision. One hour later I was playing Call of Duty and forgetting all about Maths.

*

My first period on Monday was Humanities. The teacher showed us a documentary about asylum-seekers. Most of the class were fooling around, whispering or scribbling on paper. But I was watching and thinking about last week, when we went to the café after school, and how easy and fun that was and how different my life was from the lives of most asylum-seeker kids.

*

Going home, I sat near a window on the tram. My mind wandered and I thought about going home and about some of the places asylum-seeker kids come from and all the challenges they face. My problems were stupid

Wandering

compared to theirs. My dad's a doctor and my mum's a journalist. I go to school. I have homework. We take holidays. But for asylum-seekers and their kids, life is dangerous and uncertain. This was a depressing thought. Paul Kelly was singing 'How to Make Gravy'. I turned it up and pulled out my English homework.

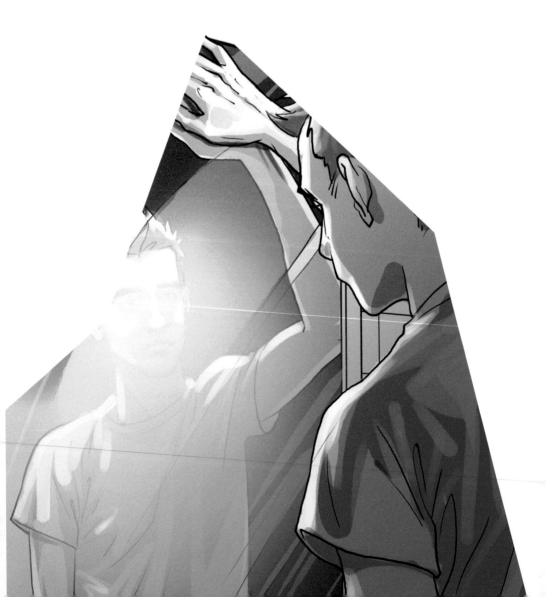

Answer Me This

Research and Discussion

1   Why do you think the author is having such a difficult time attempting to find an answer to the question about Australian identity? How does searching for the answer change the way the author perceives her environment? Give examples from the story to support your answers. Discuss what it means to be Australian as a class and agree on three distinctive characteristics that distinguish the Australian identity as unique. Was it hard to decide? Why or why not?

2   How does the author portray her love of architecture in the story 'Answer Me This'? Describe the author and her characteristics as portrayed in the story. Include how she sees herself, what she is good at and her future aspirations. Did the author achieve what she set out to achieve at the end of the story?

3   What is the reason behind the author's decision not to go on a road trip to the river? How is this linked to what happened to her older brother? Have there been times when you stood up for what you believed in and did not follow the others at school or in your life? Why? Elaborate a little more on this, talking to the person next to you in class.

Writing and Creating

1   Write a short autobiography of 300–400 words and in it describe your attributes, hopes, likes, hobbies, ambitions, reflections on childhood and a song that you feel describes you best and that you feel a connection to.

2   Use one of the following statements about Australian identity taken from the story and write an editorial about 'what it means to be Australian' for a local newspaper to be published on Australia Day. Remember to use 'we' instead of 'I' and keep it as objective as possible, as it does represent the views and the opinions of the newspaper.

   • 'To be Australian means you will be the change you want to see.'

- 'The country we live in is diverse and accepting, with complete opposites living under one sun.'
- 'Harmony and clarity are what make us stronger as people and as a nation.'
- 'Being an Australian doesn't depend on your race, background or colour. It is having respect for yourself and those around you.'

3   Prepare a class debate on whether single-sex schools are superior to co-ed schools. Use some of the information from the story to support your arguments.

Deviate

Research and Discussion

1   How does the author describe Chinatown? What connections are made between Chinatown and her identity? Provide detailed examples from the story to show the connections.

2   What is the Barden clock a metaphor for? What quality or qualities of the Barden clock are used as metaphors to describe teenagers? Who is/was Lao Tzu? Research and find information on Lao Tzu and explain his saying 'life is a series of natural and spontaneous changes' in relation to teenagers growing up in Australia.

3   How does the author describe herself at the end, when leaving Chinatown? What are some of the realisations she comes to in relation to growing up in Australia?

4   A *symbol* is what something mentioned in a story stands for, other than its literal meaning. A *motif* is a collection of related symbols in a story through which an element or an idea is repeated throughout the story. What motifs can you find in the story? Are Chinatown and the injured man motifs or symbols? What ideas or elements of identity do they represent?

Writing and Creating

1   Explain what the author means in the following sentences and how each one of these relates to a teenager's sense of identity. Consider what the writer says earlier about identity and the people she observes in Chinatown and what she says in the second statement below. Analyse and explain the differences.

   a   'So when I grow up in such a milieu, it's to be expected that a part of me will be distorted, clouded or changed on my journey to maturity.'

   b   'The faces of the orbit of people around me mesh together and I cannot make out a clear mouth, nose or pair of eyes, as all I can see is a watercolour painting of the world, with the colours running together and no defined lines and nothing to me is clear.'

2   Search carefully in the story for words with double meanings – words that are used to mean something other than their literal definitions in the dictionary.

3   In the dictionary, look up the meanings of the words below, taken from the story, and provide a synonym and antonym for each one. Then use each word in a sentence in your workbook. You may set up a table like the one shown below, giving each word a row of its own.

a   arbitrary   e   ostensibly
b   copious   f   meticulously
c   gnaw   g   deviate
d   surpassing   h   incongruous

Word	Meaning	Synonym	Antonym	Sentence

To Be or Not to Be

Research and Discussion

1   Where is the title of this story taken from? How might this saying have come to represent not only teenagers in Australia but also teenagers everywhere, according to the author? Can you think of three other famous quotes from Shakespeare's plays, that may describe and speak to teenagers even today? Write and explain these in your workbook.

2   How is the influence of Hollywood movies on the culture and identity of Australian teenagers shown by the writer?

3   How does the author create resemblances between the play *Hamlet* and her own life? What are the examples from the story that tell us this text is written and narrated by a teenager? Provide examples from the text.

4   What was the author's final answer to the question, 'to be or not to be'?

Writing and Creating

1   If you were to draw or make clips of what it means to be a teenager, which parts or descriptions in the story would you include? Draw your clips using a computer program or by hand.

2   *Intertextuality* is what happens when an author borrows something from another text, or refers to its features in some way, in his or her own text. An example of intertextuality in this story is the use of the words from Hamlet's famous soliloquy 'To be or not to be' as a title. Choose and write a narrative about teenage identity in which you borrow features from another text or texts in the same way.

3   Prepare a class debate on whether 'teenage girls are stronger than teenage boys when it comes to dealing with family grief'. Provide at least three arguments, and evidence for each argument, and use the following persuasive techniques:
    a   inclusive language   d   emotive language
    b   rhetorical question   e   appeal to traditional values.
    c   analogy

Wandering

Research and Discussion

1   What kind of a person do we sense the writer is at the start of the text? Consider what the writer says about Obama's speech as well as homework and so on. Do you identify with any of the issues the writer talks about at the start? How? Discuss in a group of three or four the similarities between you and the person in the story 'Wandering'.

2   How is the issue of asylum-seekers related to teenagers' lives in the story? Explain by giving examples from the story and from your own experiences as a teenager.

3   Read the story 'Answer Me This' on p. 69 and compare the teenage girls and their behaviour in that story to the teenage boys and their behaviour in this story. How are the two groups different in terms of teenage identity? Explain your response by providing evidence and examples from both stories.

4   Approximately how old do you think the main character in the story is? Think back to the time when you were that age. Were you feeling the same about school and other issues in life? Why or why not?

Writing and Creating

1   Find all the information about the likes and dislikes of the main character. Make a list or a collage and use it to discuss the Australian Teenage Identity or Profile.

2   Make up twenty questions to ask your classmates about teenage boys' feelings of identity. Record their answers in a table under these headings: Family, School Life, Interests and Friends.

3   Write a letter to the editor or a persuasive speech about whether teenage boys are more mature than teenage girls when it comes to real-life issues. Provide statistics and use persuasive language techniques and a persuasive tone in support of your opinion. Include your opinions about teenage or child criminals and the possible causes of criminal behaviour at such an early age.

A Clean Slate
Jessica Chisholm

'G'day Belly,' Toby says with a wink, as we meet at our corner and begin the long hike to school.

'Hey Tobias,' I reply, elbowing his arm gently. It's always been this way with Toby, ever since we were little. I guess we were kind of forced to be friends really, he was the only kid my age that lived fewer than ten kilometres away. I've got to say, though, he's grown on me from the days when he used to kick sand in my eyes.

'Well don't you look nice today,' he says in a posh voice. This was our running joke,

I always wear the same denim cut-offs and flannel shirt, and every day he comments on it in some way.

'Why thank you kind sir,' I say, imitating his accent, taking in his faded Living End tee and jeans. 'But I must say you look absolutely ridicu–' I let out a small shriek as Toby picks me up and dumps me over the fence, covering me in wheat seeds.

'You were saying,' he says, smiling as I get up, rubbing my sore posterior. I glare at him as I begin the long process of picking all the grass seeds out of my long auburn hair. I can't help but smile as he pulls me over the fence and helps me get all the seeds out of my hair. Strange how something so unkind can end up being so sweet.

*

As we near the school I begin to see my fellow school-goers, which isn't a lot of people, to be honest. Quairading District High School goes from kindergarten to year 12 and only holds about 200 people. When we get to school I find some of my friends standing in a group. I'm not as close to them as I am to Toby, but it's hardly like I can talk to him about bras, boys and beauty tips.

'Hey guys,' I say, joining the group. Don't get me wrong, I love my friends, but I've always felt like I was the odd one out. I'm not stunningly beautiful, I'm not stick thin and I don't have a boyfriend.

'Hey Bells, so what's up with you and Toby?' Becks asks as part of her morning ritual.

'Nothing. Like I said yesterday and the day before, we're just friends,' I reply, turning to find him looking at me. He winks before continuing his conversation with his mates. What was that about?

'Yeah, sure. Friends don't look at each other the way you two do,' Manda says. I feel a blush creep to my cheeks. They look at me knowingly and start to open their mouths, but the morning siren rings. Talk about saved by the bell.

*

When the final bell sounds I leap out of my seat and rush out the door. I sigh as I feel the warm breeze and the harsh sun beating down on me. I hate being stuck inside, it feels like being caged. What can I say? I'm an outdoorsy person. I end up waiting a few minutes for Toby; he was never keen on rushing. He always wants to take his sweet time, even if it means wasting mine.

'What's up, Belly?' he says, striding towards me slowly, his handsome face glowing in the sunlight.

'Not a lot. Still trying to pick the seeds out of my hair. I am going to get you so good for that.'

'We'll see. I seem to remember last time you tried to "get me back" you ended up dousing yourself in water,' he replies grinning.

'Come on! That was ages ago. I'm twice as smart now,' I say tapping my head. We chatter mindlessly until we get to the corner where we part ways.

'See you tomorrow,' I say, starting to walk away, but feeling his warm hand encircling my upper arm. I feel chills up my arm and butterflies in my stomach. Oh God, please no. I can't crush on my best friend.

'Belly, I know it's the anniversary tomorrow, and you don't like talking about her, but if you ever want to talk, you know I'll always be here.' I look into his hazel eyes, filled with worry.

'I know, Tobes,' I say softly, taking his hand off of my arm and squeezing it before walking away.

*

I look at the endless sea of gold swaying around me, like waves on the beach. The sun is setting, turning the sky a beautiful pink. I sit on the rusty tractor at the edge of the field, trying to remember the good times with my mum. I can barely remember her, even though she only died five years ago, when I was eleven. That day I came home from school yelling a greeting. Dad wasn't home yet; he was fixing the tractor. When she didn't reply I assumed she was outside somewhere, so I sat down and tried to do some homework. Half an hour later I went to the toilet. When I came out to wash my hands in the bathroom, there she was. I tried to scream, but my throat felt like it was closed. I fell to the ground, feeling my hand slip on something. I looked down, seeing the blood that coated it. No matter how hard I try, I can never get that image out of my head: her blood-covered body, lying in the bath. It haunted me.

*

I get through the next day without too much difficulty. Toby never leaves my side, which makes it easier, bearable even. When I get home Dad is sitting at the table waiting for me. I know I had a hard time dealing with Mum's death, but Dad had it even worse. He wraps me in a tight bear hug.

'I love you, Dad,' I say against his chest. Before she died our family had been distant. I'd never told either of them I loved them and whenever I hugged them it was awkward, so I had just stopped trying.

'I love you too, Annabelle, don't you ever forget it,' he says, releasing me but studying me closely.

'How are you feeling? I know this must be tough on you, Belly. Did you get the nightmares again?' he asks tentatively, his face showing both worry and sadness.

'I had one last night, but I'll be all right. Really,' I reply, knowing he has enough problems without worrying about his teenage daughter reliving her mother's suicide.

*

A Clean Slate

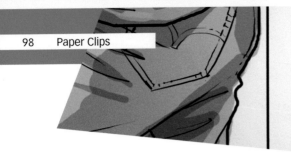

The weeks fly by after the anniversary. Soon it is harvesting season, the hottest, driest time of the year. It is in school holidays, so I can help Dad with it, as well as spend some more time with Toby. I'm still crushing on him. Whenever he's around my nervous system goes on high alert. I'm pretty sure he doesn't know how I feel, though, no matter how much Becks, Manda and Ruby insinuate that I like him, right in front of his face. I guess I'll never be good enough. Not good enough to be the son that my dad always craved, not good enough for Toby to want to date me, not good enough to fit in with the girls, not good enough for Mum to want to stay on this earth.

*

I feel my jagged breathing and sore legs, but I refuse to give up. The golden fields around me begin to blur, and I feel my head getting heavy.

'Whoa. What type of idiot goes running on the hottest day of the year?' Toby says, walking towards me, eyeing my soaking wet shirt and bright red face.

'An idiot that likes the heat,' I say, resting my hands on my knees so I can breathe easier.

'Well I'm sure …' He trails off staring at the horizon with a look of horror. I stand up straight and look to see what's so terrifying. It's worse than I could have imagined.

*

I run down the field back towards the house, oblivious of whatever Toby's yelling at me. My lungs feel like they're about to explode when I get to the house. Thank God, I think as I see Dad in the kitchen, getting a glass of water. He sees my panicked expression.

'What's wrong, Belly? Are you all right?' he asks, looking worried and tired.

'Look outside,' is all I manage to pant out before dragging his arm to where he can see the smoke that is building in the west, threatening to destroy our lives.

'Oh God,' he mutters under his breath. He studies the smoke for a few seconds before beginning to walk back into the house, yelling orders at me.

'Okay, Bell, I'm going to call the guys so we can make a plan. Go find Toby and see if he needs any help, 'kay?' I nod, affirmative, and begin to walk to Toby's. My head is spinning and I'm not sure whether it's from the running or the smoke, but I do know it's not good.

*

I get to Toby's all right to see him pacing on the porch. He sees me, then gives me a relieved smile.

'What's your dad doing? Because I can't find my parents anywhere. They're not in the house or the field or the–' I cut off his rambling by reaching over and giving him a hug.

'They went to town today, it's a Thursday,' I explain into his shoulder. I hear him breathe a small sigh. We go inside with nothing to do but worry and pray.

*

Within ten minutes I can see the fire. Not good, so not good. Our paddocks are drier than a dead dingo; it'll only take a matter of minutes for it to get to us. I hear water bombers overhead as Toby and I hastily make our way over to the school, which doubles as an evacuation centre. Along the way Dad joins us. I've never seen him so sad, so resigned. We walk into the school gym, seeing all our neighbours and friends. I know we're all about to lose our livelihoods.

*

We stay in the gym for what feels like hours, listening to the crackles and bangs through the doors. When we are given the all-clear to go outside, my breath hitches and I begin to cry. There is nothing left, no golden crop, no family homestead. Nothing. I feel an arm around my shoulder and look up expecting to see Dad, but instead it's Toby. We both just stand there looking at the charcoal, wondering how life is going to go on. We've lost everything. But at least I have my family and friends. Only now that I've lost everything do I realise how much they really matter. I pray to God that the fire wasn't just to teach me a lesson. I slide my arm around Toby's waist and pull him close. Without hesitation I turn to look at him and give him a peck on the mouth, praying it doesn't backfire. The best way to start again is with a clean slate.

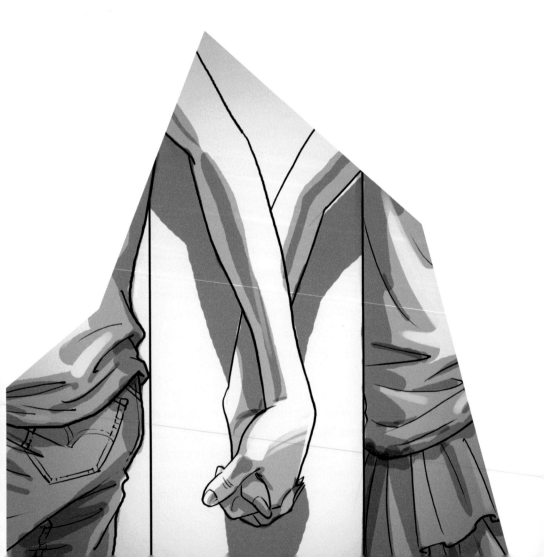

Well, Whatever
Alexander Sirian Be

Where am I? Where am I going? Who am I? What am I doing?

Some questions never really go away, not when you have the luxury to sit down and really think, and really listen to another person. It's disquieting sometimes when you can't find the answers, don't know what or how or when.

Though it's infinitely more unsettling when you realise for that moment what the answers are.

The whole weight of your existence overpowers you and you feel insignificant, incapable of human response; your feeble mind cannot even begin to resist. And yet even with all the power of that moment, all the incredible swirling energy of the universe that expands inside your tiny chest and fills you with the chaotic indifference of the ether, people still pass you, eat, drink, laugh, have sex, piss, moan, cry, vomit, die, live, as though your moment is completely and utterly irrelevant. This is the closest you have to ever leaving something, creating your legacy, your significance, and it's almost laughable how little anybody cares.

Well, whatever.

I'm going to claim my splinter of importance in this life of fading moments and obnoxious dreams. I will attain the most of what it means to exist as Avowka Siik. Remember that; that's important. I didn't say human, or person, or homo sapien, I said my name. Guess why. No, you wouldn't understand; it's because every moment, every person who's died, the millions of stars exploding and millennia of evolution all lead to this second, and if even the slightest bit was different, then my name would be something else, my thoughts something else, my language something else. So my name carries significance, then. It is the result of tireless, immeasurable evolution and we're all bound by the laws of a science that wouldn't even make sense to any sentient life form except people: physics.

Consider this: the moment you roll a die, the number that will come face up is predetermined – based upon the force of your throw, gravity, the lifespan of the die and the environment. The moment you release the die is the moment it has already begun dying; its fate has been set. So what separates us from the die? We are born in a certain way,

surrounded by an environment that permeates our subconscious and then our conscious, and then brutally forces us to conform, to believe a certain doctrine, and to behave like people and deny our animal roots.

And the fact is that eventually the greatest equaliser – the universe – will claim everything, including us. It's just how it is. We can't attribute emotion or indifference or callousness to it. It just is, and it just does what it does. Much like the die, each moment of our lives from the moment we are born has been determined by the chance of birth. From then on, each experience, like each bounce of the die, is just a part of the process, and the number the die comes up with – our survival rate – is zero.

So how can we have the impertinence, the self-assumption, to attach significance to a life that is so momentary and so naked in the presence of an observer that lacks any human qualities that would allow our inanities to matter? When we live in a city so choked by its own ignorance and by its self-absorption that it cries out for exposure only to be stared down and withered by its very own eyes – the media – how can anything short of arrogance make us think our lives are significant? In every Melbourne street that we wander through, we feel a sense of emptiness, a lack of fulfilment in those who pass by, and an inherent wrongness in the very culture that we live and breathe.

This is a world where those who wish to stand alone against the overpowering voice of the prevailing culture are slapped down. We have no exposure, no examples to show us how a better world would look. How can we start to create such a world without first knowing what it smells like, feels like and looks like?

Yet this is home, and for whatever reason – human attachment, inanity or irrationality – we are bound to it. We are bound by love, by security, by hate, by blood, by disgust and by beauty. In Melbourne there is an enchanting sense of youth and powerful energy, energy that is naive and yet also grounded by pragmatism. It is not yet corrupted by the careless decay of complacency or suffocated by its own assumed importance. It is clean and proud of itself – proud enough to retain its endearing qualities when confronted by the leering, smirking, manipulative faces of other cultures.

It is in this city that I, and so many others before, with and after me, will have begun their journey towards significance. It is a woeful, temperamental and whimsical journey, bound by the fickle nature of the human heart and the so very human tendency to overcomplicate things. Many have abandoned their journey, distracted by the baubles and trinkets that lie by the wayside. They have done this before me and with me, and will most certainly do so after me. I, Avowka Siik, too cannot be infallible – far from it. Yet I have a definite, firm belief, stemming perhaps from arrogance or from my earliest beginnings, that I will take, and make mine, my own significance and fulfilment. This, however, remains to be seen. I am immature and not yet ready to seize the reins. I still lack the qualities of control and power, which are rooted in self-understanding and the conviction of a set of beliefs.

We are all like passengers, each on our individual ship that we had no hand or choice in building, yet each of us chooses our own direction and navigates the waters as best we can. We have the choice either to look up in amazement at the world around us and decide where we will go, or to doggedly navigate our vessel through churning waters, only to realise that we have only ever known our own ship and never bothered to learn the wondrous gift of joy that is living.

Your hair is ragged, soft, your skin prickling with anticipation. Your stomach threatens you with overload as your heart hollows and collapses on itself. This is a moment you will remember for the rest of your life. This moment will shape the person you will become. This is shatter point one. There are people like hurricanes who fly and whirl across your life and alter its course. They're the ones you can't hope to ever match; they vibrate on their own capacity, with strange knowledges unknown by anyone but themselves, so far and foreign. Some part of them, no matter how you may seek to love and own them, physically, emotionally and spiritually, will always be bound to no one and no thing. But the force of their pure, ecstatic wrath is a pleasure none can hope to withstand. Every moment spent in their mad presence is a beautiful despairing. And in this moment you dare to claim the tortuous pleasure

Well, Whatever

of one of these human hurricanes, hands gripping the handrails, every ounce of barely contained energy charging towards your metaphysical construct. Sweat lightly covers your skin and you hate the heat; you hate the way you can't bear to move no matter how uncomfortable you are, but it doesn't matter. You don't care. This comes to your attention and is lost, dwindling to a fraction of a fraction of itself.

You're staring at a goddess, divine and chaotically powerful.

You're staring a goddess into willing submission, your breath on her face, her scent making its way into your brain; the ultimate aphrodisiac. Her body is indefinable and perfectly flawed. May you remember the moment you took and bent the hurricane, the goddess, to your will. You lean closer, desiring the hazy pheromones, mad, drunk, intoxicated with the presence of a power you suddenly understand you could never have stood against. And in your hubris, in all the whirling of the hurricane, you touch lips with her. Hair crackles with electricity, hearts thunder with weakness, the world surrounds you with intense colour, and everything and anything is wrapped and absorbed by the combined power of the moment and cataclysmically exploded from your heart. And the energy contained within you in that moment could freeze time – capture anything, nothing, everything, all. Even with this hurricane the moment is brief, yet that's all one can ever ask from such a chaotic, dominating creature.

You know this because she returns your kiss. You know this because she wants to stop herself and your breath stops. You know this because she takes up your lips again and you can feel them, heavenly pale red.

This is possession, this is ownership, this is primal, base desire that cleaves through 'civilised' construction. This is love; this is beyond linguistic representation; this is beyond knowing, grasping, understanding.

This is phase one of significance.

Love.

Miss Letaya-Kirra
Keeley Roberts

I was sitting at the bench having breakfast with my two younger brothers and we were munching our food. Unexpectedly, Mum came out saying she had something important to tell us all. We all went quiet as she told us the shocking news – that she was pregnant.

Being the eldest, I was used to Mum telling me everything, or even telling me important stuff before the boys. I was shocked that she hadn't already told me about this. Mum was taking precautions, so I thought it was a lie. Before she told us this news I had always gone on about how she should have a baby and how I would love a little brother or sister, but when it actually happened I was shocked and not even excited. It felt weird knowing she was pregnant.

Instead of being happy, I was angry and annoyed at her all through the whole pregnancy. I didn't even touch or feel her stomach through it all. And sometimes I would just ignore Mum and not speak properly to her for days. I went to a few ultrasounds with her, but mostly I just acted as if it was all fake. Twenty weeks went by quickly and I decided I would go to the ultrasound appointment that would find out if Bub was a girl or a boy. Seeing little hands and feet on the screen seemed so unreal but when the doctor said the bub was a girl, I got a feeling both bad and good. I love babies and I had always wanted another younger sister or brother, but knowing that I was actually going to have one felt weird.

The weeks went so quickly and Mum couldn't do as much stuff as the time came closer. I began to help cook tea, go shopping and help with my brothers. Her final and last week of the pregnancy came quickly and was even more intense. Mum became angrier and moody, which always made me angry back at her. She went to her last ultrasound appointment at the hospital the day Bub was due but had not come yet. The doctor said she could come any time.

So that night when we were all sleeping, Mum's waters broke at 1 a.m. I was woken up by her ten minutes later and she told me. Shocked and not ready for the experience, I got up, got ready and got my brothers up too. Mum was a bit stressed out and tired and had sharp pains, so we called her friend to pick us up. The boys got their bags, which they had

packed a few days before, and they were picked up and taken to a friend's house. I went in the car to the hospital with Mum and Mum's friend Donna. The trip to the hospital was very quick as Mum's friend drove as fast as she could on the Southern Outlet.

Arriving at the hospital, I ran in to get a wheelchair for Mum. The nurses came down to get her first and Donna and I got all her bags and stuff for Bub out of the car. Walking up the stairs to the third floor and walking to the room they put Mum in was a bit scary, knowing that very, very soon my baby sister would come into the world. We finally found Mum's room and saw her lying on the bed. I watched everything from start to end. Donna held Mum's hand and I watched my baby sister come into the world. I had planned to cut the cord, but as I saw her head come out the doctors noticed she was looking purple and that the cord was wrapped around her neck twice. A shiver of fright went down my back as I watched my sister being pulled out and realised she wasn't breathing. I didn't ever think it would get that bad. I ran out of the room crying, because it was so terrifying knowing that my sister wasn't alive and knowing that she could stay like that. I waited outside the room and then I decided I would go back in. Watching the doctors work on my sister with all the different machines and new technology was terrifying, but then it was all quiet and suddenly she started crying. It was a relief knowing she was fine.

The doctor called me over to where she was and told me to touch her gently. I didn't want to because I was terrified that she was going to die again, but I touched her. She was adorable. I then put her first nappy on and a cute little hat, wrapped her up in a blanket, then held her. She wasn't even crying. I took photos of her and then the doctors had to take her from me to get her properly checked out in the Intensive Care Unit. Mum, on the other hand, didn't know what was going on. She didn't get to hold her daughter and she was still in shock. I sat down and had a little rest and waited and waited. About two hours later they brought Bub back to us and we named her 'Letaya-Kirra'. We didn't get to see her for long; they had to take her back to Intensive Care because she wasn't

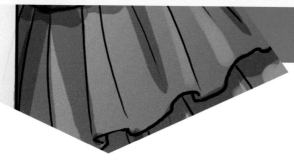

well. I went home to get my brothers and bring them in to see their newborn sister. They were really excited to see her, but sad when I told them what had happened. They saw her in the Intensive Care area, but no one was allowed to hold her as she was unwell. I took the boys home and we stayed at a friend's house for the night, as Mum didn't trust us at home by ourselves. The next day Mum was let out of hospital, but we had to leave Letaya.

Day by day we went to see her, from 9 in the morning to 9 at night, spending as much time as we could with her. Five days later she was allowed to come home. As excited as we were, we kept calm. Bathing her and dressing her in her own tiny clothes was amazing. It didn't even seem real that she was alive, nor that she was so close to coming home with us. But it was real. We gave flowers to the Intensive Care nurses and said a big thank you for keeping Letaya safe and well. We took her home with us and the journey began.

Day by day it got harder for Mum, with bottles to clean and make up and dirty nappies to change, Letaya to wash and clean, spewy clothes to wash and dry every day. I helped a lot and got used to the routine. Sometimes I got woken up at 3 a.m., but apart from that she was a good and healthy baby. She slept a fair bit, and I got quite attached to her and used to helping out. As a few weeks, then months, went by we all became more familiar with everything and things became easier. She grew up so fast, grew out of her clothes so quickly. Seeing her start to make sounds with her mouth and start smiling, and laughing when we tickled her, just amazed all of us.

Sometimes I get angry and annoyed, as she is the only one in the house that gets all the attention, but I still love her. Now, as she has just turned six months old, our whole family has amazing experiences. She is starting to crawl, and can walk in her walker. Since the first moment I saw her, I'm always being surprised as she grows up. I already have so many memories. I've taken her out with me for the day, taken her to see my friends, she's been swimming and I look after her when Mum goes out. I'm mostly looking forward to bringing her to child studies with me

Miss Letaya-Kirra

at school next year. I now know how to change her nappy and wash and dry her, I pick out her clothes and dress her, I know how to make her bottles, feed her, burp her, put her to sleep and feed her solids.

Letaya-Kirra, now six months old. Born 22 April 2012.

Yes, I will always love this miracle princess. xo

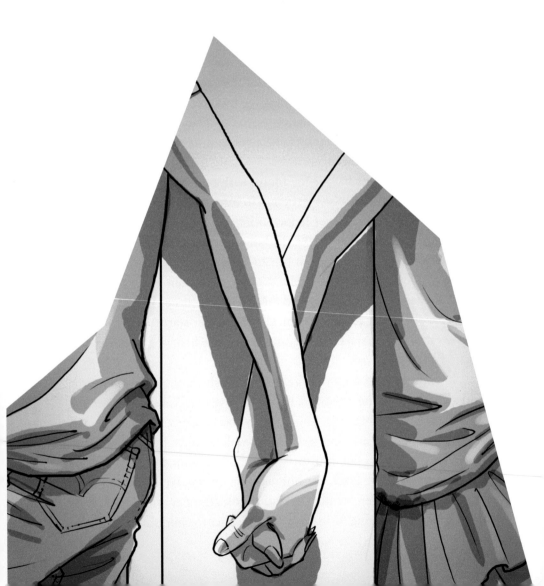

My Own Little Ponting
Milan Kantor

You never expect that it's going to happen to you. I hear sad stories all the time about relatives and friends dying, but I never think much of them other than how hard it must be for the family. I guess I got this from my mum – she's always managed to take funerals in her stride. I never imagined it would be this hard, though. There is truly nothing you can do to prepare yourself for the moment.

I once did a task in school where we had to write a pretend eulogy for someone that we knew. I joked around throughout the class, never thinking for one second that one day I might actually have to give one, especially not so soon. It was school that kept me away from my brother's death, but I don't regret that. School also gave me my last memory of my brother, and it is school that will let me cherish it forever.

The last time I saw my brother he was smiling at me outside the bus window, standing by my mother's side. He was in his cricket gear, ready to go from the station to the oval and play with his friends. My whole family had come to see me off for what would be my last term at school. He was upset; it was obvious, but he tried to contain it. That was one of his best traits; he was a lot stronger and more mature than other boys his age but he was still just a kid, young and innocent.

We had spent the night before playing a magical game he'd invented in which he was Harry Potter and I was Ron Weasley, even though I had an English essay that was still missing everything except its title. My brother managed to create imaginary worlds of his own and share the joy of them with those around him so easily that I often found myself skipping work to play with him. Whenever I walked him down to the milk bar as a toddler to get our favourite ice-cream, everyone would stop and take the time to tell me how beautiful he was. On the odd occasion when someone would walk straight by, we would circle around them until they noticed his delightful smile and energy.

My brother was going to be the next Ricky Ponting. Everyone around here aspires to be that at his age, but the difference with my brother was that he had the determination to get there. In his life he had already experienced a lot more then those city boys ever would. After Dad left

and I headed out to boarding school in the city he was the little man of the house, looking after our mum and little sister. That was a lot for him to deal with, but he did what he could to help out, learning how to shear the sheep and helping the shearers on the weekends. He also mowed the neighbour's lawn, trying to save up for the newest PlayStation game, which I often had to buy for him so he didn't fall behind on what was hot in school. He picked up football and cricket at school and had shown enough natural talent to eventually make it in life. He had many more skills as well, but never the opportunities to follow them through.

I will miss my brother. This much I'm sure of. I feel an absence in my heart, as though a big part of me is missing. I don't know if that's possible, but I feel like it's gone. My life, and the life of anyone else who knew him, will never be the same. He was truly, and always will be, my own little Ponting.

A Clean Slate

Research and Discussion

1   How old is the main character and which school does she go to? How does she meet Toby? How does she feel when she first arrives at the school and speaks to a group of other friends? Why?

2   What does Annabelle's father do for a living? How did she find out about her mum's death? How did this change her relationship with her father? Why do you think she feels she is not good enough? Give examples from the story.

3   Do you think the narrator is in love with her long-time friend, or did she merely need someone when her mum passed away and he was there at the right time? Provide three examples and evidence from the story to prove that this is the case or otherwise.

4   What makes Annabelle cry at the end of the story? How does the fire affect the love between the two friends? Why? Provide evidence and use your own words to answer this question.

Writing and Creating

1   Imagine you are Annabelle and going through hard times coming to terms with what has happened. Write a letter to your mum some time after she passes away. In your letter, share any emotions that you were never able to talk about with her, and tell her how much you love her by also mentioning the things you did together and the things you still wanted to do in the future.

2   Write a second part to the story, five years in the future. Include the same characters and add two original characters. Use dialogue to show the relationship and the love between Toby and Bells.

3   Write a short story about love using the quote from the story 'Only now that I've lost everything do I realise how much they really matter' as your title. Use a circular narrative structure and include figurative language tools such as metaphors, similes and vivid imagery. Your characters need to be original, as well as the plot, and you must have a message about love in your story.

Well, Whatever

Research and Discussion

1   The writer is exploring the important meaning of life and existence. Why does he mention physics? How does he explain the relationship between human beings and a die that is thrown? Do you agree? Explain your answers by providing evidence from the text. Discuss your views on life and existence and how physical and spiritual forces predetermine these.

2   How does the writer relate success and life to Melbourne as his home and its culture? What does he mean by 'We are all like passengers, each on our individual ship'? Discuss the difficulties and advantages one would experience in a city like Melbourne in terms of achieving their dream in life. Do you think the location we live in, or our home, determines our future? Why or why not? Explain by giving examples of ideas from the text.

3   How is the writer's description of love different from any other descriptions you know? What does he mean by 'hurricane'? In what ways does this hurricane affect the person? Use the information in the text to support your answers. Discuss as a class his description of love and its significance in life. Do you agree, or is it impossible to agree? Why or why not?

Writing and Creating

1   The Macquarie Dictionary Online defines the meaning of love as 'A strong or passionate affection for another person'. Write a 500–600-word expository/informative article on 'A teenager's guide to love and life in the twenty-first century', in which you describe these issues from a teenager's perspective. Include examples from your life and from other people in your life.

2   Using your dictionary, find the meanings of the following words, taken from the text, and place each of them in the correct category (noun, verb, adjective, adverb). Fill out as much of the rest of the table as you can. See the sample entry in the table opposite.

a   endearing   c   callousness   e   pheromone   g   hubris
b   infallible   d   baubles   f   whimsical

Noun	Verb	Adjective	Adverb
infinity	–	infinite	infinitely

3   Using the same 'ship' metaphor as in the story, write a script
    for a speech you will give to year 7 students about 'true
    friendship'. Give advice based on your life experiences and/or
    the experiences of people you know.

Miss Letaya-Kirra

Research and Discussion

1   Why was the writer disappointed at first and angry and annoyed later by the news of her mum's pregnancy? Discuss the jealousy and the treatment of children equally in a family. Do you think parents have a big role in sibling jealousy? In what way? Does this affect the way the siblings feel about each other even when they are adults? Provide examples from your life and the text you have just read.

2   How did the writer's mother feel towards the last few weeks of her pregnancy? Do women go through psychological changes during and after pregnancy? Research and find out the diagnosis of such changes. Do fathers also go through a psychological phase during and after the mother's pregnancy?

3   What was so frightening for the writer? What was the complication with the delivery of the baby? Do you think sibling jealousy is really evidence of their strong love for each other?

Writing and Creating

1   Write a 450–550-word entry in the writer's diary on the night of her baby sister's birth. Include all her feelings before and after the birth as well as her feelings about her other siblings. Remember to include a date, time and place for your entry.

2   Rewrite the story from the mother's point of view in 600–800 words. Include your feelings, using figurative language, imagery and appeals to the five senses as part of your descriptions of the hospital, your children and the new baby. Add a father to the mother's story and explore their relationships with all the children.

3   Working in a group of four, design a 12-question survey on butcher's paper to find out whether the individuals in the survey really love their siblings or not, whether they are jealous, or whether they would help their parents as an elder sibling. Include a key at the end of your questionnaire and scores for each level. Each student in the group needs to contribute *three* questions and describe one of the levels out of four levels in the key.

My Own Little Ponting

Research and Discussion

1   What point about death and eulogies does the writer make at the start? How does he feel about his brother's death? Have you ever felt that you will never fully understand the painful experience of someone else, or vice versa? Research the seven stages of grief an individual is said to go through after the death of a loved one. Are the stages universal or culturally determined?

2   Describe what kind of person the writer's brother was, as he portrays him. What was special about him? Do you think eulogies reflect the real person, or do they mostly mention positive aspects? Why? How does this relate to the story?

3   How does the title relate to the plot of the story? What themes apart from death can you identify? Provide examples and evidence from the story for each theme and discuss with the person next to you whether they identified similar themes, then share your findings with the rest of the class.

Writing and Creating

1   The narrator and his family live in rural Australia. Write a report of 400–500 words about his brother's death for the local paper. In your article, answer the following questions:
   a   What happened?   d   When did it happen?
   b   Where did it happen?   e   How did it happen?
   c   Who was involved?

2   Find where the adjectives below were used and use another adjective to replace each one without changing its meaning. You can *only* use another adjective, not a noun or a verb. Remember that you can convert verbs into adjectives by using a gerund.
   a   beautiful   b   delightful   c   mature   d   pretend

3   Write a second part to the story in 600–800 words in which the writer's brother returns home. The writer is still the narrator but the title is 'The Imposter'.

Home
Catriona Cowie

My mother stands watching me through the window.

I turn and stare back.

She does this every week, every shift, every ten minutes remaining of my four-hour workload selling books to strangers with false smiles and pleasantries I don't mean.

'Have a good day' (but not really).

When Mum slides through the closing doors in the last few minutes of retail, I treat her as a normal customer; refuse to acknowledge we're part of the same past, the same future, the same 'now'.

'Your grandmother is dead.'

'I'm sorry,' I say, my expression blank. But inside I am keeling over. I am crumbling. The nightmare climaxes and I am surprised that there are no zombies, no werewolves, no gigantic beasts; only death.

I hand her a bag, even though she hasn't bought anything, and recite the famous line wishing her a pleasant evening.

Mum leaves the store and returns to her usual spot, waiting for me to finish. I tiptoe away from the counter and nod at my manager as I brush past, grab my bag and exit the store. I can never get away fast enough.

I bump into my mother and feign surprise.

'Mum, what are you doing here?'

'I don't want to play tonight,' she says, her eyes wet. She dabs at them with the bag I gave her and clasps my hand, running a finger over my thumb, trying to comfort me. I twist our hands around so that I am the one consoling her, one stroke at a time.

'I'm sorry,' I say again, acknowledging our encounter at work. She smiles with fakery I recognise from my own deceiving, and I let her get away with it, for she is happier this way. 'Come on,' she says. 'Let's get doughnuts.'

The doughnuts are delicious. All gooey and jammy and icing-y. I hold my stomach in as Mum reverses the car out from the underground carpark (it's too hot this close to Christmas to park in the sun) and I sacrifice one hand to reach across and hold hers. She smiles, and although the rims of her eyes are still red, her smile is real and so is mine.

Home

We get home and find the cat sitting on the front steps. He meows at us and I pick him up and bring him indoors. He's not going to be allowed out again for the remainder of the night; we're protecting the possums or something, not that he'd be able to catch any.

My brother Richard is plonked upon the couch, watching the football and pretending to know what is going on. He cheers at the screen, but even I, someone who doesn't know anything about sport in general, can tell that nothing of real value is happening. My family is adamant about introducing Australian values into the household now that we've completed our citizenship. They forgot to give us a plant at the ceremony, though, so I'm convinced we're not really Australian.

There are used tissues strewn over the coffee table and I grab the wetted bag from under my mother's fingertips and shove the tissues into it before placing it in the bin. Richard ignores me and I think that he should expend his sadness in a form he actually enjoys. I don't say these thoughts out loud.

Mum has disappeared, and I follow her voice out into the back garden. Smoke blooms into the air as Dad stands silently burning the sausages, and his willpower, as Mum shouts into his ear. They cost twelve dollars, she says, they cost twelve dollars.

I don't care for the taste of sausages, or kangaroo, or meat pies. I'm vegetarian. Not because I believe in preserving the lives of animals (they're dying for a good cause, the ads say), but so I can be served first on school camps. I used to hate the tree-huggers finishing their food before me. Now I'm one of them.

I tiptoe through the house, enter my room and land face first into my pillow. I spend the next five minutes scrabbling around in my pocket, trying to get out my headphones and iPod, but when I do, the music does not calm me. It's all brass bands and strange soprano singers with warbly voices chanting about the rain and the woods and the picket fences. I feel like I'm there now, in my mittens and wet hair, dancing on the moors like Cathy and Heathcliff.

'It's me, I've come home,' I whisper, wetting the pillow with saliva. I fish out *Wuthering Heights* from my ever-expanding bookcase and immerse myself in that world – a world filled with hatred much more than my own. I only read Brontë's work of fiction to convince myself that Britain is not where I want to be; it's awful and it's tiring and it's heartbreaking. It doesn't always work, though. And as I set the book aside and move in the general direction of where the sound of my name is coming from, the Australian heat chokes me and I want to go back home.

Mum has set the table and we all sit down simultaneously in the spots we've occupied these past few years. Mum places a burnt veggie burger upon my plate with a pair of tongs and even though I haven't asked, she answers, 'Your father'.

I want to scream 'Why is "your father" an answer? Is his existence the *only* result of the Big Bang, or "God's" creation? Why must you always put us down?' Instead, I cut myself a large piece of the blackened matter, which cannot possibly be called a veggie burger any more, and swallow it whole. It jams in my throat as I try to smile at my father, and although I am choking it feels like the right thing to do. I am closer to feeling this way. I am closer to my grandmother.

SpongeBob on crack dances in front of my eyes and my laughing only makes the choking worse. My mum has disappeared from view, and I feel a hand slap against my back. I yell out in pain, and travelling along that yell is the chunk of burger now detached from my vocal canal. It arches through the air and straight into the kelpie's mouth.

'Good boy,' Richard says, unfazed by the spectacle.

My eyes burn red, either from exhaustion, or from anger at my own life; yet whatever conclusion Mum comes to, she sends me to bed with a cup of tea in my hand.

I prop the pillows up and get comfortable, body heat escalating from the doona worn by sweat, and the steaming liquid tickling my throat.

I ponder upon life and death and birthing and topics I would never talk about with my friends until I reach her, my grandmother, the one

Home

not allowed to rest in her grave until we have performed the ceremonies we feel necessary to mourn her. I slide my oily fingers together and pray to a God I do not believe exists that she is fine, that there is more after the final drop of the eyelids, but I know it is no use. I know there is no sense thinking upon death when life is so short, and I know that as much as I want to be philosophical and find the meaning of life, it is not what she would have wanted. She would have wanted my complete and total happiness.

And so I slide *Wuthering Heights* underneath my bed and focus my gaze upon the Union Jack waving in the humid air. But rather than gazing upon it with lust for my country, I rather think how beautiful it looks, side by side, hand in hand, with the Southern Cross.

'It's me, I've come home,' I say.

And this time, I have.

It Will All Be Worth It
Amie Rovacsek

'What's wrong with that boy's arm, Mum?' A young boy stared and pointed at me from across the shore.

'Honey, don't stare,' the mother replied.

At first I found these gestures rude and hurtful, but I grew to accept them as a normal part of my day. After all, it's not every day you see a one-armed teen. I haven't always been like this, though; in fact it has only been within the past year that I have been a freak show. I'm Steven, the fifteen-year-old, one-armed ex-surfer, and this is my story.

*

Every Saturday morning I would get up at 4 a.m. to meet Sammy and Nat at Cottesloe. We would be there by 4:30 and be well and truly riding the waves by five. Every Saturday morning until 18 January 2011, that is. I woke up that morning just as I did every other weekend, keen to get to the beach. But I never imagined that would be the last time, in a very long time, I would feel the waves crashing around me, smell the fresh sea air and go surfing with my two best friends.

We hit the water a little earlier than usual that morning, which at the time we didn't think was a big thing. It was still kind of dark, but we didn't want to wait any longer. The waves were amazing! Better than any I had seen for the past few months. We wasted no time; we were out pretty far riding the biggest waves we could, having a great time, until we saw it.

Before I had a chance to react it was under my board. I tried to jump up but it was too late. It already had hold of my arm. I tried to scream but not a single sound escaped my mouth; there was already a lot of blood. It thrashed me around like a rag doll. I was queasy and light-headed; everything hurt and the only thing I could see was a sea of redness – my own blood, I presumed. I could tell I was slowly losing consciousness. I could feel it slowly being pulled away, further and further until all the pain was gone and I could hear nothing but the beating of my own heart.

*

'Steven?! Steven don't leave me, just keep your eyes open, open your eyes, man.'

'They will be here soon, just hold on Steve, they're going to help you, you're going to be okay, please hold on for us,' my friends begged and pleaded but it was no use. I had lost so much blood, they might as well have been talking to a corpse.

*

I woke up what felt like an eternity later; my entire body ached, especially my arm. It was throbbing but I had a strange feeling of emptiness. I looked over to discover the cause of the feeling. My arm was gone!

What was left of my arm was covered in bandages. The nurse walked in and asked me how I was feeling. I lay there with a dumbfounded look on my face. 'I'm missing an arm! How do you think I feel?' I exclaimed.

My mum walked into the room. 'You're awake; how are you feeling?' she asked.

'I have one arm, for godsakes; *you* get your arm eaten and tell me how you feel! The shark may as well have just killed me, I'm never going to be able to surf again, my life is basically ruined.'

With all the commotion the doctor had decided to come and see what was going on. 'Steven, how are you fee–'

My mum cut him off. 'I wouldn't if I was you.' The doctor checked my vitals and explained what had happened since I had arrived at the hospital.

'Luckily the surgery went really well, and with the right rehabilitation you should regain full movement in your arm.'

'What arm? This thing?' I pointed at the stump. 'This is useless. You need arms to surf, arms with hands, like two of the things. Not one and some stupid stump!'

'Steven, these people saved your life; without the surgery you would be dead right now.'

'They should have let me die. Surfing is my life; without it I am nothing.'

The doctor interrupted me. 'Well, actually, it is still possible to surf; it will be a challenge and it will take a lot of hard work, but it is most definitely possible.'

If I could, I would have jumped up and hugged him right then and there, but for obvious reasons that wasn't quite possible. 'Really, I can surf again?' I asked with joy.

'How about we get through recovery before we worry about surfing?' Mum said.

'Like I said, it won't be easy, and there are still no guarantees your arm will heal properly, but it is looking pretty good at this stage.'

With everything that was going on I had completely forgotten about Sammy and Nat. 'Where's Sammy and Nat?' I asked.

'They're at school. I think they're coming back this afternoon,' my mum replied.

Sure enough, later on that afternoon I was visited by my friends. They explained the entire story and filled me in on everything that had happened after I'd passed out.

'You saved my life!' I exclaimed.

'Meh, it was nothing, you would have done the same if it was either of us,' Sammy replied.

'So when do you get out of this hole?' Nat asked.

'Wednesday hopefully, and trust me, Wednesday can't come soon enough.'

Wednesday eventually came and I couldn't have been more relieved to leave the hospital. I was still in a lot of pain, but my arm was healing really well. I had to go to physiotherapy twice a week and before long I could move my arm, what was left of it at least, as much as I could before the attack.

*

Finally the day had come. Today was the day I found out if my arm had healed properly. Today determined whether or not I could go back to the water. I had what felt like a herd of elephants stampeding inside my

It Will All Be Worth It

stomach. I felt sick with both nerves and excitement. I had never been more anxious in my life. Nat and Sammy had agreed to come along. As we sat in the car on the way to the doctor's, the sick feeling grew. I tried many times to imagine my life without surfing; it was an image I did not enjoy at all. Finally I didn't have to imagine any more.

'It looks great, Steven. Your arm couldn't have healed better.'

I almost cried with joy and relief. I had never been happier in my life. All the dreadful thoughts of never being able to surf again were gone; it was like a huge weight had been lifted off my shoulders.

'So you keen for the beach this weekend?' I asked my friends on the car ride home.

'How about we try the swimming pool first?' my mum said nervously.

*

Three weeks later I went to the beach for the first time in almost six months. I had never been happier to see the bright white sand, the crashing blue waves. Mum, on the other hand, had never looked more terrified.

'I've already had one arm eaten by a shark. What's the worst that could happen, Mum?'

'You still have one more and two legs,' she replied.

'Mum, I will be fine, I promise.'

I made my way to the water. The waves crashed over my feet and suddenly it was too much. I began to feel queasy. The smell of blood filled the air, my legs turned to jelly, the image of my almost lifeless body being thrashed around like a rag doll flashed before my eyes.

'I – I can't do it,' I trembled,

'It's okay bro, it's just too soon, we will get there eventually.' Nat put his arm around my shoulder and walked me back up the beach.

'What if I can't? What if I can never go back in the water?'

Sammy grabbed my hand. 'Look at me. You can do this; we will do it together.'

*

And he was right because here I am, swimming at the very beach where it all happened. I still haven't actually been surfing, but I can tell the day will be coming very soon. Sammy and Nat have stuck by my side the entire time. They even found, and introduced me to, a girl who went through the same thing as me, and she's been teaching me a few techniques to help paddle out and to pull myself up with one arm. Training and rehabilitation have been gruelling and both mentally and emotionally draining, but I know that eventually it will all be worth it. The day I can finally dive into the waves and become one with my board and the water, it will all be worth it.

It Will All Be Worth It

Up in the Stars
Samantha Go

The atmosphere grew dim with coldness as the wind wrapped its icy touch around everything in its path. As Elena stood, the chill ran up her spine to her neck with its frosty breath. She shivered with discomfort as the day grew darker and more sinister. She did not have the cheerful company of the birds that had perched in the trees, nor the hint of sunshine that had penetrated through her skin and into her heart, filling it with happiness and warmth. Even when the sun was out, it would not take away her misery, not any more. The trees slipped away into a space that light could not reach. It was the world's time to sleep and be calm, but not for Elena. Elena was wide awake with a plan that she had been working on.

The rough, crisp leaves below her crunched as she ran. Her awareness was alert to countless small alarms. She glanced in every corner, cautiously scanning the dark silhouettes that surrounded her. A sharp sound startled her. She could feel the presence of something nearby. Elena peered at the grey tones around her, focusing on the apparent depth of the landscape masked by the dark. She studied the stillness of her surroundings for any slight movements. An owl that had woken slowly lifted its wings and flew up and out of her view, creating ripples in the air and starting a breeze that touched her shoulders. Her chest collapsed quickly as she let out a small sigh of relief. Regaining her confidence, she wandered further into the bush.

The small beads of sweat that trickled down Elena's nose shimmered as the moonlight cast its magical glow on everything around her. She could feel the rugged texture of the trees as her hand brushed the foliage. Small strips of bark extended like chaotic pieces of hair slightly curling up at the ends. The bag she carried on her arm had almost slipped off, but she managed to pull everything back up and into place.

The uneasy atmosphere reminded her only too well of the survival horror game she had been playing on her Nintendo. Elena could picture herself as the game's heroine. At any moment she might be confronted by a deadly monster – the kind with a bulging figure and an arm that had the strength to kill a player with one hit. The thought of it reminded her of how close she had been to losing her console after her mother had tried to take it away. Elena remembered standing threateningly over her mum and demanding that she give it back. 'Stupid idiot,' laughed Elena as a playful grin appeared on her face. She was satisfied with her control over her mother.

She looked ahead and realised that her sense of direction had failed her and that she had gone the wrong way. Calmly, she tried to figure out where she was. As she kept walking, she felt fairly certain of where she was heading. According to her judgement, Glosons Creek should be there. She hoped that her calculations were wrong and that she wasn't going to come up against the creek, but as she came closer she could see the water right in front of her. Her hands fidgeted at her sides and her feet shuffled forward, tiny piles of dirt building up at the edges of her thongs. Elena sat herself down by the creek, which prevented her from going any further. She let out a deep sigh of frustration as her head sank into the nest provided by her hands.

'Why? Huh? I am totally sick of this. Every time! Life has to always screw me up!' she screamed angrily. In her fury, she swung her foot forcefully into the creek and the water splashed into the air and fell back. She cursed as she put her foot on the ground. Elena lowered her heavy sports bag onto the dry soil and threw down her backpack and other belongings with it.

Her pocket glowed and her phone started buzzing. As she withdrew it from her pocket the brightness illuminated her face and blinded her vision. Her eyes squinted as she looked at the screen. 'You have 1 message' read her phone as a continuous mail symbol flashed on the screen. She was expecting a text from her friend after asking him if she could stay at his house for a while, but as she opened the message her smile faded. 'Elena please come back home. I'm worried. I love u dearly Len. Please tell me you're safe. xoxo Mum.' Elena shrugged and deleted it. 'Leave me alone. God, I can take care of myself,' she said under her breath. She had given up on her plan and decided to sit there until she could be bothered to move. What could she do now? She was stuck.

Up in the Stars

A few minutes later she had calmed down. She dipped her finger into the water and watched the way it responded to her movements. As the tiny ripples spread outwards, her eyes watched the reflection of the sky in the creek. She slowly lifted her head and saw the tiny specks of glitter scattered across the sky. A sudden rush of emotion overcame her. Her hair clung to her face and she could not hold back the tears in her eyes. Her face crumpled and creased with emotion as she raised her head.

As she gazed up at the stars, visions of her past resurfaced. She could not escape this time; at last the world had her attention. It finally hit her like nothing she had ever experienced. A part of her that she had locked away in a dusty corner of her brain for a long time was being swept out into her view.

She remembered her father and all their times together. She could picture his gentle face watching her as she ran in and out of the ocean. 'Watch out, the waves are gonna get you!!' his voice echoed in her mind. She could picture them on the beach when she was only five. They would sit there and build sandcastles until eventually the waves would creep up and push the sand into the ground as if there had been nothing there at all. As the breeze from the ocean cooled the air they would lie down and eat hot chips. The seagulls would frolic one by one, each eyeing the crispy golden chips. Elena would get up with her hands firmly placed on her hips and her eyes glaring intimidatingly into theirs. She would chase the swarm of seagulls until they all flew up like balloons released into the sky. She remembered the salty smell of the water and the piles of sand she involuntarily took home with her in the depths of her pockets.

She also remembered playing cricket at her Aunty Jack's house with her cousins. The sweet victory of winning the game always gave Elena a sense of pride. The sun's rays would gently highlight her wavy brown hair as she baked in the oven-like atmosphere. The kookaburras would perch in the gum tree that shaded them from the heat in Aunty Jack's backyard. The smell of sausages and meat lingered in her nostrils as the barbecues were fired up. She would always sneak around and gobble a few sausages before they were presented to everyone and her

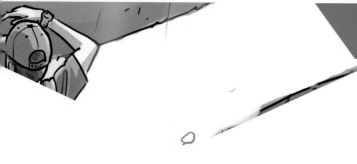

dad would always have to take extra precautions because he was aware of her cunning tactics.

Memories of the time she camped with her parents also came back. Her mother used to tell her stories of the adventures of a bear named Woodsy as they sat around the fire. Elena's eyes would gleam every time Woodsy found a solution to his problems. She recalled the warm, sweet feeling of being held in the arms of her father at night while they looked up at the stars. Being in the arms of her father had given her a sense of refuge from all evil and, more, a sense of belonging – something she no longer felt in connection with the world. She had loved to wrap her small delicate fingers around her father's big hands as they cuddled each other tightly. 'Elena, I love you my dear possum. When I leave this world, know that I'll always be here, watching you from the stars above. I want you to be your best and take care of Mum, okay?' whispered his voice in her mind. He had pressed his lips against her head and kissed her gently, inhaling the sweet aroma of flowers that scented her hair. His time was limited; he had had a massive battle with pancreatic cancer. After a while, his body could no longer fight it. This had changed Elena.

The place Elena felt she was now stuck in was the very same place she had been in when she shared that last precious moment with her father. As more memories came rushing back, she knelt on the dirt and the tops of her thongs dug into the soil. She clenched her hands and she looked up to the sky with remorse.

She wished so hard that things could be like that now. The sparkling stars looked like elongated blurs of light in her tear-filled eyes. She looked up at them and spoke from her deepest being.

'Dad … I'm so sorry. I'm not your perfect, little possum, but right this instance I know that I should change, and I am willing.'

Vivid memories of how she had fallen behind in school and the pain she had inflicted on her mother came back, haunting her with guilt. Everything that she'd wanted, her mother had provided. But nothing was ever enough. What was meaningful happiness? Elena did not know. She was never satisfied with life, but it had been so kind to

Up in the Stars

her even though she was not so kind back. She didn't want to be that person any more.

'What have I done? She doesn't even deserve it …' Elena wailed and her voice faded into the silence of the night. Her eyes shut tightly for a few seconds as she assessed what she had become after her father had passed away. Her back hunched over and her hands rubbed into her damp face as memories of all the pain and suffering she had caused rushed in to poison her like venom straight to the heart. Elena could finally see the reign of terror she had inflicted on everyone around her and it was surely, to say the least, unforgivable. Guilt ate her away with every second that the world gave her.

'Elena!' her mother called faintly in the distance. Elena looked over her shoulder and saw a small light flashing through the trees. She abandoned her things and raced into the woodlands, following the brightness of the torch. The light moved from side to side like a lighthouse checking for ships that were in trouble. Elena was one troubled ship seeking forgiveness.

Elena found her mother panicking. 'Mum … I'm so sorry for everything,' she said. They embraced each other tightly.

Darkness
Hugh Offor

It was dark. It was always dark. Whenever I opened my eyes I could see nothing but darkness. I shifted in my bed and moved my feet to a different spot. I could hear them, my thoughts and fears whispering in my ears. Something moved. I froze and held my breath as I lay rigid as a board. I slowly moved my hand towards the lamp on the bedside table. In a rush I flicked the switch and sat up. Nothing was there. I was safe, for now.

I think I'm perfectly normal, by most people's standards. I work hard to keep that guise up. I don't know what people would think if they found out about my fear of the dark. It's not entirely irrational. Fear of the dark has been around for pretty much as long as the human species, but it is not needed as much these days. It's a survival instinct that helped our ancestors survive the night. If they were on the alert they would notice if a snake or some other animal was sneaking up on them. As children, most of us outgrow that fear. I wonder what all my friends would think if they knew ... they'd probably just laugh at me.

My school is nice enough. It's got nice people, nice teachers and plenty of things to do. I'm not exactly an A student, but I get by. Anyway, when I came to school on Thursday, I knew it wasn't going to be good. I had several assignments due later in the day and I had spent all of yesterday afternoon hanging out with my friends. I trudged in gloomily, already dreading the detentions to come. I placed my books on my desk and slouched forwards. It was going to be a long day.

I felt relief as the bell announced the end of class. I grabbed my books and shoved them into a makeshift pile. Just as I was about to step through the door I heard a voice.

'Dale, please don't leave just yet.' It was Mr Watson, calling me from across the room with one hand raised.

'You didn't hand in your assignment, Dale,' he said. My heart sank. I had managed to conveniently leave the class when we were handing them in.

'See me at my office after school today, please,' he told me. 'You may go.'

*

I was waiting outside Mr Watson's office when it started. Thunder echoed through the corridor. Classroom windows shook and a teacher stuck out her head, then shrugged and returned to work. I looked around nervously before checking my watch. What was keeping him? I wondered. It was starting to get dark outside and the last of the sun was blotted out by dark storm clouds. Suddenly the lights began to flicker. The building began to shake as thunder rocked the evening. Abruptly, the lights failed. I was plunged into darkness. My breathing rate sped up. I began to panic. I squeezed my eyes shut and curled up into a ball on the floor. When the lights suddenly came back on, a student in my class found me lying on the ground, crying and terrified.

*

The story spread like wildfire. People stared at me and whispered to each other as I passed them in the corridor.

'Did you hear about that kid there?'

'No.'

'When there was a power out on Thursday he panicked and was lying on the floor crying!'

'No way!'

'Yes way!'

No one ever looked at me the same way again. When I saw any of them outside school I hung my head and tried to avoid being noticed. 'The Incident' had destroyed my practically non-existent reputation. Whenever I answered a question or said anything in the classroom, I could see people smirking and remembering my story.

*

It was dark again. Something moved. I didn't know what. It didn't matter. I closed my eyes and felt a tear trickle down my cheek. I lay there, silently crying, for the whole night. I wallowed in my misery for hours. In the morning I was so tired and my throat hurt so much from crying that my mum refused to let me go to school. I hadn't told her about what had happened and about how everyone saw me. I thought she would overreact and tell me to face them. I would just get laughed at.

*

I had to face my fear. I had been talking myself into it for days amid the rush of homework as our end-of-year exams approached. If I went out there and faced it, the next time I was alone in the dark it wouldn't seem so bad. So I made my plan.

*

I waited till school was over and walked home. I lived quite close. When I was most of the way home, I stopped at a park by the road and settled down with a book. I would wait here till dark, then walk past the small park and into the paddock beyond. My town was so small it went from town to farm right after the buildings finished.

Night fell. I picked up my bag and jumped the flimsy fence. I walked out into the field. I couldn't see the lights of the town any more. I turned around and faced the darkness. Crickets chirped around me and small frogs in the nearby dam called out into the night. I looked up at the sky and saw the stars sparkle. I sighed and smiled quietly. It was beautiful. With a grin on my face I turned around and walked back towards my home.

Darkness

Home

Research and Discussion

1   What is the sad event underlining the characters' feelings in the story? How did this event affect the protagonist? How was she handling the grief caused by this event? Provide examples from the story to support your answer. Are there different ways of dealing with grief in different cultures? Research the ways in which different cultures mourn death. Provide examples and compare these with the way this is done in mainstream Australian culture. Discuss your findings with others in class.

2   How do we know that the protagonist was not born in Australia? Give examples from the story. Explain how the protagonist feels about being Australian at the start and at the end. In what way are her feelings different?

3   Why does the protagonist have the book *Wuthering Heights* in her bookcase? Research and find out about the themes and characters in *Wuthering Heights* and link these to the protagonist's feelings about it in the story.

Writing and Creating

1   Think of the person in your family that you relate to the most. Write a profile of that person, describing them in detail. In your profile include:
   • a general description of this special person and how you relate to them (is she/he your mum, dad, friend, niece …?)
   • reasons why you admire this person more than others. What qualities separate them from other people?
   • examples of ways in which this person shows these qualities.

2   Write a 400–500-word orientation to the story 'Home' about the protagonist's life before her grandmother's passing. Include her school life as well as her family life before coming to Australia, as well as how she feels about home.

It Will All Be Worth It

Research and Discussion

1   Describe the incident that changed Steven's life in the story. How did the incident influence him physically and mentally? Research and find similar incidents, how those people's lives changed as a result of them and how they dealt with the incidents and their influences on their lives.

2   Discuss with a partner the possible lessons to be learned from the story 'It Will All Be Worth It'. What can one learn from Steven's experience and other people's similar experiences in life? Use the meaning of the title and examples from the story to discuss and support your ideas and opinions.

3   How important were the reactions of the people around Steven during and after the incident? Explain how his family, and in particular his close friends Nat and Sammy, helped his healing process.

Writing and Creating

1   Write a script for an inspiring speech Steven is asked to give at the year 11 assembly at his high school two years after the incident. In his speech include the advice he would give to other teenage surfers and victims of sports injuries. The title of your speech is 'Riding a Dream'.

2   More golfers are killed by lightning than swimmers by shark attacks in each year. However, humans kill 100 million of these endangered species a year.
    Organise a class debate with affirmative and negative teams and an adjudicator. The debate topic is whether 'sharks and crocodiles should be killed following attacks on humans'.

3   Steven describes the feeling he had during the incident thus: 'I had what felt like a herd of elephants stampeding inside my stomach.' What kind of figurative language example is used in this sentence? Explain exactly what Steven means by this. Find five other examples in the English language of similar descriptions involving animals. Use them in a sentence. Start with the one related to the location of butterflies.

Up in the Stars

Research and Discussion

1   What is Elena planning to do at the start of the story? When and how do we find out? Are the issues portrayed in the story, and what Elena is going through, considered common among teenagers? Research statistics about teenagers leaving home. What are the main reasons why a teenager may make such a serious decision?

2   Why does Elena change her mind? What are her regrets? Why does she feel guilty? Provide evidence from the story to support your reasons. Do you ever wish to spend some time alone to think over issues related to you, your family and your decisions in life? What are some of the issues and decisions that you find difficult to deal with? Discuss and compare these as a group with others in the class. Record the most common issues and decisions and report back to the class with your findings.

3   What happened to Elena's father? How does she remember him? Do you know anyone who has lost one of his or her parents? How did they cope? Do you get along better with one of your parents than the other one? Why? Explain this with some links and examples from the story 'Up in the Stars'.

Writing and Creating

1   A eulogy is a speech written to praise someone or something highly; in particular, someone who has just died. Using all the information in the story and your imagination, write the script for the 400–500-word eulogy written by Elena, which she reads at her father's funeral. In Elena's eulogy, speak about the vivid memories mentioned in the story, and the stars. Describe her father from her perspective and tell how much he meant to her and what her feelings were for her mum and her family.

2   Using the descriptions of the memories in the story, design four memory clips of Elena (in table format or in a short video clip) that portray her memories of her father as well as how she has lately treated her mother. You can use a computer program or draw by hand and include speech bubbles.

3   Explain the meanings of the sentences below in your own words.
    Find any figurative language techniques used and finally identify
    the emotions described and whether any of these relate to
    common teenage issues.
    a   'Her face crumpled and creased with emotion as she raised
        her head.'
    b   'Being in the arms of her father had given her a sense
        of refuge from all evil and, more, a sense of belonging –
        something she no longer felt in connection with the world.'
    c   'Vivid memories of the pain she had inflicted on her mother
        came back, haunting her with guilt.'

Darkness

Research and Discussion

1   Why is Dale worried at the start of the story? What is the scientific term for Dale's condition? Find other kinds of fears your classmates may have. Discuss the consequences of such fears in their lives and how they can overcome them. What kind of fear is *hippopotomonstrosesquipedalian*? Find the root of this word and explain its meaning. Do you know of any strange fears that someone else has? Do you think some of these fears should not be considered phobias or be taken as seriously? Why? What are the criteria for labelling a fear as a phobia? Research and report your findings back to the class.

2   Explain the incident at school. How did it affect Dale? Provide evidence from the story using your own words. Do you believe Dale could face and overcome his fear in a different way? What would you do if you were in Dale's position?

3   In the end, Dale is able to face his fear after a long night of crying. What is the message the author implies in the story? Why didn't Dale tell his family about the incident at school?

Writing and Creating

1   Research and find information about a common phobia and present this information in an article (500–600 words) or a 3–4-minute PowerPoint presentation. In your article include subheadings for sections on the historical background of the phobia; the effects of this phobia on people; statistical information from the world and Australia; and the cure for the phobia, if there is one.

2   Use words from the story to design a crossword puzzle. In your puzzle, include questions or sentences and their meanings as well as comprehension questions related to the story. An example would be 'What is the surname of Dale's teacher? (6)'; 'The scientific name of Dale's phobia (12)', etc.

3   Search the story and find:
    a   the simile about Dale's movement when it is dark at home
    b   the metaphor about how Dale reacts when the lights go out
          at school
    c   the metaphor about the speed of the news of the incident at
          school
    d   the alliteration used in describing the fence.

SUNBURNT
COUNTRY

Mallee Trees and Red Dust
Teagan Brandis

'Teagan, can you come and help me, please?' my dad summoned me from outside. I got up from my post in front of the fan and opened the sliding glass door, letting a wave of forty-degree air through the flywire.

I walked over to the chookyard, where my dad's voice had come from. I went to where he was crouching down next to a scratchily dug hole underneath the chicken wire.

'That blasted fox has been into the chickens again and this time he's taken my best laying hen. I called Uncle Max and he said to bury chook wire underground all around the perimeter of the chookyard so he can't dig his way in. I need you to hold up the wire while I attach it to the original wire. Okay?' he said.

'Okay,' I said as I rolled my eyes. Dad was usually at war with this fox. It was always breaking into the chookyard, harassing the sheep and killing the lambs and Dad would retaliate by setting fox traps and fox-proofing the chookyard. Dad always said that we kids gave him white hairs from stress, but I'd started to think it was that fox.

When Dad wasn't in battle with the fox he was the town gardener; planting trees, looking after the gardens, mowing the town tennis courts, raking leaves, spraying weeds and looking after his pride and joy – the local cricket pitch.

When we'd finished with the wire he looked pleased with himself.

'Let's see him try to take my chickens now …' he muttered as he ambled to the fridge to get a beer.

He really needs a better hobby, or he's going to turn into one of those crazy old men that sit on the front porch in their rocking chairs ready to shoot anything that moves with their 12-gauges, I thought to myself.

*

My name is Teagan Brandis, I am fifteen years old and I live in Nungarin, Western Australia, about 270 kilometres north-east of Perth. It's in the central wheat belt and has a population of around 120 people. It's pretty isolated, but every school holidays we get a few tourists. We have a local

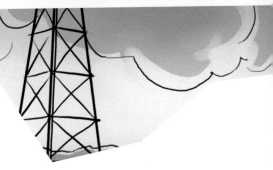

pub and the haunted McCorrey's Hotel, and one of my older brother's friends has lived in both of them. We also have a local pool, tennis courts, a bowling green and only a primary school. This means that every morning my sister Zoe and I have to travel an hour to Mukinbudin, just to go to high school.

*

I woke up with my alarm clock beeping at me saying it was 6 a.m.; saying it was time to get up. I walked out to the chookyard and opened the wire door. The chickens were startled on their roosts and started fluffing up their feathers in a huff. I emptied their food and water bowls over the back fence and filled one bowl up with food scraps and the other with water from the tank. I rummaged underneath the hens for eggs and placed each egg in a plastic shopping bag whenever I was successful in finding one. I was thankful that the flies were still asleep in the trees at this time because the chookyard is fly central, thanks to its rotting smell. I'd rather have Vegemite toast for breakfast than a swarm of flies.

*

I walked out of the house ready for school and closed the flywire door. The clink of the door alerted the dogs. My two kelpies, Gypsy and Piper, bounded up to me and lay on their backs for a belly rub, writhing with excitement the whole time. Our old bitzer dog (bits of this and bits of that) Darcy plodded at her own pace towards me, panting as she did so, clearly annoyed at the fact that she couldn't keep up with the other two any more. They were all panting from the heat and whimpering for my attention. I gave the kelpies what they wanted and Darcy a scratch behind her ears.

*

The old school bus drove down the long rust-coloured road to Nungarin Primary and then to Mukinbudin High School. It flew along, kicking up clouds of red dust into the air behind it. My mum has been the bus driver ever since I was a kid and she used to play my favourite tape on the way to school – The Hooley Dooleys – and all the kids on the bus had to listen to it.

*

During class everyone would sit in the air-conditioned classroom drifting in and out of boredom-induced sleep brought on by our teacher's monotonous drawl of pointless facts. At recess and lunch everyone would seek refuge in the shade, fanning themselves with their homework books and trying to shoo the flies away from their food so that they could take a fly-free bite. When school was over everyone would go home and collapse once again in front of the fan, too tired and overheated to do anything else.

*

Every weekend my dad would take me and my sister Zoe out driving around the paddocks on family land in Mukinbudin. Our dad takes us driving because my mum isn't game enough to go driving with me. I personally think that I'm not that bad. Maybe she thinks that I'm going to crash the car because I'm clumsy and take after her. Or maybe it's because she doesn't trust me with the keys to anything after I accidentally locked us out of the house during a dust storm when I was five and no one's let me live it down since.

All of a sudden there was a loud bang off in the distance that echoed through the trees, sending galahs and twenty-eights squawking into the air in all directions.

'Follow the sound,' my dad ordered Zoe, looking worried. She jolted the car into action and did as she was told.

When we came around the bend to the paddock with the windmill we saw the shapes of two four-wheel drives poking out from behind the salmon gums. My dad gave my sister a swooping hand signal telling her to speed up. When we got closer we saw two burly men walking over the mallee roots carrying shotguns. An orange, furry lump hung over one man's shoulder.

'Stop!' Dad ordered Zoe. She stopped the car with a sharp jolt. My dad reached under the seat and pulled out his 12-gauge shotgun and two bullets, which he loaded into it. He opened the door, slammed it shut and strode over to the men, cocking his gun as he did so. When the men noticed him they dropped the fox and held up their guns in self-defence.

'This is private property,' shouted my dad, 'have you got permission to be here? Hunting?'

'Yes,' stuttered one of the men.

'From whom?' asked my dad. The men paused for a second at this question.

'From … err … Jack,' the other one said.

'There's no Jack in this family. Get out!' Dad yelled, waving his gun in the direction of the nearest exit. 'And don't let me catch you hunting on this land again or I'll shoot you like you shot that fox.'

The men got in their cars and blasted their music, throwing out empty beer bottles and profanities as they drove off.

My dad walked back to the car, put his shotgun away and went around to the back of the ute. He came back with a shovel.

'I'm going to bury the thing. Wait here,' he said as he walked off with the shovel over his shoulder.

*

We never saw the men again and we never saw Dad's fox again, at our house anyway. We learned that it had walked all the way to Mukinbudin to my great-uncle Max's farm and had worked out how to pull the yabby nets out of their dams and steal the bait for itself. Oh well, I guess it's Mukinbudin's problem now.

Room to Grow
Maya Simpson

I don't like moving house.

We had to move. My grandparents had died and left us their farm. Dad said it was the perfect opportunity for us kids to live somewhere nice. I thought London was nice.

So we left London for some small Australian farm by the sea. I was pretty sure it would be terrible.

*

I walked out of the Perth airport into the blinding Australian sun. Inside it had been cool and air-conditioned, but outside it was hot and dry. There were flies everywhere. I felt pretty stupid as I waved my hands around, trying to rid myself of them.

It was a four-hour journey to the farm. Jacob, the farm helper, came to pick us up.

'Hey there,' Jacob said. He shook our hands. His skin was darker than mine. I wished my skin was darker. I wanted Jacob's accent too. Riley began pestering him with questions.

'Do they have electricity there?' the pesky ten-year-old asked.

'Of course they don't,' my older brother Aidan teased.

Riley believed him. 'Really? What about telephones?'

'He's joking, Riley,' I said. ''Course they have electricity.'

'And phones?'

'And phones,' I replied.

We stopped at a roadhouse for lunch. We sat on picnic benches near a bird aviary and ate hot chips. Dad said the birds were galahs. At home we had service stations, not run-down roadhouses.

*

The farm wasn't too far from the town.

'You kids can walk to school,' said Mum.

Aidan pulled a face at me. I laughed. The farmhouse wasn't too bad. But it was only one storey, which surprised me. At home we'd had three.

Dad said he was going into town to find something to eat.

'Anyone want to come?' he asked. I decided that would be better than unpacking, so I agreed. Riley came too.

We passed farms, wineries and sea. Our farm was on a hill, so we could see the sea easily. There was so much space. There was room to grow.

*

The town wasn't too bad. It was quite large and there was a bus that could take you to the nearest city. I could go shopping. I felt better. We drove around, looking for somewhere with takeaway food.

Riley wanted fish and chips, but we had eaten chips for lunch so we settled for Thai. The food made us really thirsty. There was a rainwater tank out the back of our house. I decided that rainwater tasted nicer than the tap water in London.

*

It was the summer holidays, so we didn't have school. It was crazy hot, though.

Dad showed us every little part of the farm. He took us for long bush walks, climbing over huge rocks. We would sometimes walk to the beach and go swimming and exploring in caves. Riley made friends with our neighbours. He and another kid called Jack became close friends.

I spent as much time in the sun as possible, hoping to become tanned like Jacob. It didn't help that Mum made me put on so much sun-cream that my skin practically shone.

Jacob was teaching me Australian slang. It was quite fun, actually. Aidan said that was stupid but I caught him several times, listening behind one of the ghost gums that grew thickly around the house. Dad made Riley and me check the water troughs every day to make sure the cattle had plenty to drink. Sometimes, if we finished quickly, he would let us stop to swim when we were done. Dad, Jacob and Aidan had to move the cattle to different pastures. They rode the horses and Jacob rode his motorbike. He said he would teach me how to ride it too, but Dad wouldn't let me help with cattle moving. At home Dad let me do everything. I missed England.

We started school. They start high school in year 8 here, not 7, so I was stuck with another year of primary school. I made new friends, but I missed my friends in England. I wanted to go back home.

*

In late summer, Jacob kept the water tank on the truck just in case one of the paddocks caught fire. Dad said this was stupid and Jacob shouldn't worry. Jacob said it was better to be safe than sorry and refused to take the tank off. Dad said he was just being stubborn.

My best friend at school was Mia. Mia, Riley, Jack and I would take big buckets and go berry-picking. Mum told us we weren't allowed to come home until the buckets were full. This took hours because we ate so many of the berries. The blackberries were best. They were next to our neighbours' winery and their dog chased Riley for ages until his owner, Ethan, called him off.

'Sorry 'bout that, mate,' he grinned, taking his dog's collar and helping Riley down from the tree. They both looked at the three of us. We could barely talk, we were laughing so hard.

'I … didn't know … you were scared … of … dogs!' Mia could barely talk through her laughter. Riley glared at us.

'I'm not scared of dogs!' Riley grumbled. 'Only massive Rottweilers that try to attack me.'

'Bluey's no Rottweiler!' laughed Ethan. 'He's an Australian cattle dog. Blue heeler.'

I laughed and was rewarded with a punch from Riley. 'Shut up Charlie, that dog could've eaten me! Did you see those teeth? Massive!'

'Bluey won't eat you.'

'He ate our chooks last week,' said Jack. 'He could've got you mixed up with one of them.'

Riley wasn't having a good day.

We made iced chocolate with ice-cream when we got home and drank it sitting on the edge of the pool with our feet in the water. Aidan came out.

'There's a fire!' he cried breathlessly. He sounded like he'd been running. 'Where's Mum?'

'In the laundry.' I felt worried. A bushfire?

He left. A minute later we heard Mum. 'Do they have the water tank? Call Ethan, he'll help. Quick!'

She slid open the back door. 'I'm going to drive you to Mia's, all right? It's fine with your parents, Mia, I checked. Jack, I'll drop you home too.'

'Will the fire reach the house?' Riley asked.

'I hope not.' Mum looked worried. 'Pack a bag each, okay? Hurry!' She really was stressed.

Mia followed me to my room.

'Don't worry, we get bushfires up here all the time and everyone helps out,' she said. 'It probably won't burn your house. It might, but it's unlikely.'

'Great, thanks for that,' I said sarcastically.

'No worries.'

'Charlie, you packed?' It was Riley. 'Mum wants everyone in the ute.'

'Okey dokey, we're coming.' I zipped up my bag.

*

It was exciting being evacuated to Mia's. We spent the afternoon eating icy poles and watching TV. There was fish for dinner. We peeled potatoes for chips while Riley watched cartoons. Mia's dad took a beer out of the fridge.

'Do you want me to chuck the fish on the barbie?' he asked. I love barbecues.

Mum called later to say that the fire was out and we could come home tomorrow. It was fun staying with Mia, but I would be glad to be home. I liked the farm nearly as much as England. Dad decided that we should keep the water tank on the truck all year. Jacob found this hilarious.

*

Autumn arrived. I missed summer, spending endless days in the pool, at the beach and the water park with friends, learning to surf and watching Aidan come first place in the surfing competition. Also, I had just got my skin to a nice, brown suntanned colour and I didn't want that to go away.

I made Vegemite sandwiches for our school lunches. Riley watched me carefully over his bowl of cereal so he could make sure I didn't put too much Vegemite on his sandwich. Aidan came in and took the last piece of damper from the bread bin. 'One of them for me?' he asked, grinning.

I nodded and added an Anzac biscuit to each lunch.

'You gave me the smallest one,' noted Riley.

'Who cares, you …'

'Mum! Charlie's calling me names! And she gave me the smallest biscuit.'

'What? Shut up you dobber. Fine, I'll give you a bigger biscuit. Happy?'

'No. Can we have lamingtons too? Mum made them.'

'Why don't I just give you a whole cake?' I said sarcastically. Riley took me seriously. 'Okay.'

Aidan laughed and took the lamingtons out of the fridge. Aidan and I had never been very close in London but now we would do heaps together.

Nearly every day we would ride our horses through the fallen leaves by the orchard. Sometimes I beat him. The cows began to calve and we had to check them every day. Mia and I went riding in the rain one evening and we found an abandoned calf. We kept it by the wood stove to keep it warm. Jacob brought an old cat's bed for it to sleep in. We called him Bambi and fed him from a bottle. One day Dad said that one of our neighbours' calves had died and we could give him our calf to adopt. I told him that wouldn't work, but Jacob said that if we put a jacket made out of the dead calf's skin on our calf, the mother would adopt him. Maybe. We didn't want our calf to go.

Jack, Riley's friend, also lived on a farm and at butchering time our dads helped each other with their jobs. I didn't like butchering. I had

Room to Grow

NAPLAN testing now too, and with all this going on I realised how much I missed London. I had been so busy over the summer enjoying myself, I had forgotten.

Some mornings we would wake up to find the entire farm covered in fog. We always got up early and ran around in it. You couldn't do this at home. We would play in the old rusting tractors that had been in the one place for years. There were no more late summer storms, which were always a relief after the summer drought, but it was still exciting to have winter storms. Once, lightning hit one of our trees and the whole house shook. After the storms we would go riding through the water. Aidan and I would sometimes ride our quad bikes and I was learning to ride Jacob's bike too.

We got a new puppy. Not a blue heeler. Riley was still scared of them. Sadie was a chocolate-coloured kelpie. She was beautiful. We spent hours training her up. She was a herding dog, but she was also a great pet.

Mum got sick of cooking for us, so she made a huge pot of pea-and-ham soup and we had to eat it every day for a week. Jacob said he would never touch pea-and-ham soup again. I couldn't help but agree.

Winter came and went. Mia and I would ride our horses under the clothesline and grab onto it. Confused, the horses would stop running. We can't ride horses like this in London.

Dad took the horses and us down to the beach and we rode in and out of the waves. Dad said we were becoming pretty good riders now. Sometimes we would take our dinner with us and eat it by the sea. It was getting warmer and we could play under the sprinklers now. The water park opened and my friends and I went nearly every week. Jacob made us a cubby in a tree by the chicken coop. Sadie tried to round up the chickens whenever she got into the coop. She never ate them, but it sure sounded like it.

Summer came again and school ended. I had never had such a hot Christmas. I would be starting high school now, in year 8. I didn't really care. I didn't talk to my old friends much. Their lives seemed quite different from mine.

I love Australia.

Saying Cheers
Jaimee Rich

Only we know what it's like here, down under.

No pictures or words could describe her fierce deserts, remarkable coral reefs, breathtaking landmarks, strange animals, rebellious bush-rangers, dramatic climatic range or wild bushland. We're different, with our 'G'day mate' and 'snaggers on the barbie'. Our Chrissies aren't white; we have boomers instead of reindeer and sand instead of snow. The history of the white people was invasion, not evolution. We're born for the hot, sandy beaches, endless summers and clear blue oceans. And at the end of the day, how could we be any luckier? So on 26 January every year, we all take time out to say 'Cheers' and we call it Australia Day.

I tread along the hot sand, the colour of red earth. It doesn't burn my feet, not any more. In odd places you may find a coolibah with a roo enjoying its shade, or a feathered fella darting across the lonely plains, his long legs covering three metres in a stride. It's the daily norm for Nymagee. The sunrays reflect off the clear water of the billabong – so appetising, that cool fresh water. In the near distance are my rotting glossy planks, creaking jarrah floors and thin wooden door frames, all making up the old cottage I have lived in since I was just an ankle-biter. I can faintly make out the swing of my old man's axe cutting up the firewood. Mum's hanging out the washing on the clothes hoist; not too long from now she'll be out there again in this heat. The sand doesn't get any cooler before I get to the front door. I push it and I hear that eerie creak as it opens.

'Where you been, girl? Probably sulking about that city boy again, hey? Gee, fifteen-year-olds these days, they drive me nuts! You're about as useful as tits on a bull, you know; we never gonna get these decorations sorted!'

Overwhelmed by my sister's abrupt 'greeting', I quickly make my way over to what seems like just a big mound of plastic rubbish. There are faded blue flags including half a Union Jack; dusty toy koalas; old banners missing the 'S' and 'L's from 'AUSTRALIA' and not in the slightest good nick for our Australia Day celebrations this evening. Jenna snarls at me as I get up to walk away.

'Not so fast, you slacker. I know the deco's nothing flash but it's better than absolute jack. If you're not gonna help me, go see what Nanna's done with the food.'

Sisters ... who would really want one?

I'm quick to duck off to the kitchen; the whiff of golden steak pies and smoked lamb chops is so alluring. There's nothing like Nanna's Aussie Day specialities. Laid out are bowls of fresh cut salads with red onions, crunchy lettuce, red ripe tomatoes; a rainbow of oranges, apples, watermelons, kiwifruit, blueberries, strawberries, raspberries ... Over to the right of the kitchen is a dish of macaroni cheese and coleslaw salad, and to top it all off is my most favourite: the barbecue meats. The smell of the cooking beef snaggers and the sizzling steaks tickle my tastebuds and my stomach groans, longing for them. Nanna grins at me, noticing my obvious affection for her miraculous meal, but not even offering a little taste.

'Sorry chook, not till the evening.' And she shoos me away.

After a short while sitting around, twiddling a cocktail flag between my fingers, I glance out the window to watch the first of the guests roll in. A cloud of red dust smothers their brand spanking new ute. Uncle Jerry, Bradley and Susie get out, greeting Dad with a loving hug, muttering words of adoration and fondness for our country. I am standing in the hall as they barge unceremoniously through the door. I greet my uncle and Bradley with a light cheek peck, but Susie just rolls her eyes. We all know where she'd rather be on a Saturday night. Bradley all of a sudden begins excitedly rummaging through his satchel, pulling out some red rocket-like objects. I can't believe my eyes – they're fireworks! We're having our very own skyshow! Everyone lets out shrieks of excitement. This is no doubt going to be a ripper 26th of Jan!

Bradley's done the New Year's Eve fireworks down at the footy oval for a couple of years now. He'd have had to fork out for a licence for this party too and Mum wants to give him money for it, but he won't take it. 'Late Chrissie present for everybody, Shirl – we're all square!'

The tunes of Men At Work blast loudly from the stereo and everyone is singing and dancing along, especially to 'I Come from a Land Down Under'! By now aunts, uncles, cousins, friends and locals have arrived from all around, creating a sea of denim shorts, 'I Love Aussie' singlets and thongs. The kids wear masks of face paint and red, blue and white tats from the newspaper, showing the true Aussie spirit. Garden lights line the border of the billabong to illuminate it under the night sky as twenty little tykes splash, dive and giggle from its waters. I look up to the eucalypt and meet two beady eyes staring straight at me; this poss is DEFINITELY not ecstatic about all the noise. The adults dance and laugh to the best of AC/DC, Midnight Oil, Silverchair and even some Paul Kelly, a stubby in hand. I really wouldn't be anywhere else. Eight o'clock strikes and everyone's digging the sausage sizzle. Plates and plates of macaroni, salad and chops are handed out, and by the time the whole meal's been conquered all are trudging around with big, bulging bellies. This night is just how every 'cheers to our country' should be.

And just before it's all over, everyone takes a seat on the soft red earth and the first firework explodes in the air, its magic captivating every eye in the crowd. I find myself letting out a stupid grin, really hoping nobody sees. I am truly having the time of my life.

And you know I could be out partying hard, getting drunk, hooking up; but my country, my home means much, much more. The battered decorations, hot dishes and fresh fruits, the traditional tunes, the laughs and giggles are no brilliant bash, but it's the way she would like it, our Australia; the way it's meant to be.

So here's to her tonight.

Thank you, my sunburnt country.

Saying Cheers

Christmas Stampede
Matthew Hill

My boots crunched on the dry, dead grass. The sunset was casting shadows over the fence posts that made them look like skyscrapers. I turned to look at my dad. He was finishing tagging the last cow. He turned to me with his old cracked face and said, 'Michael, give us a hand over here!' I sighed and shuffled over to help him; it sucked that I had to do all this work. It wasn't fair that everyone else lived in the cities with all their friends, relaxing and doing nothing, while I was stuck on this depressing cattle farm. And to make matters worse it was almost Christmas, which meant twice as much work to get all the cows milked, cleaned and fed. On the farm it definitely isn't a season to be jolly.

*

Later I asked, 'Dad, do you think that this Christmas we could take a trip into Perth and stay with Mum for the weekend?'

'Absolutely not. There's just too much work to be done on the farm. Besides, I bet this Christmas is going to be the best one we've ever had.'

He walked off into the shed while I sat down at the TV thinking about what he'd said. Why was Dad always so content to stay on the farm? Didn't he know that there's so much more to be seen? And what did he mean when he said that this Christmas would be the best, when we always do the same old things: eat a turkey, watch the cricket and open some presents? Don't get me wrong. I like Christmas with Dad, but sometimes I just wish something more exciting would happen.

*

Christmas time in Australia is always hot, especially in Perth. Some may call it a problem, but others think it's good because you can go to the beach with your friends and family. I've never been to the beach and I have no friends out here, so I hate summer more than any other season. I used to have a friend here once; his name was James. We used to do everything together, but one day he had to move because his dad was offered a job in the city. I still think about the fun we had. We always used to go into town and sneak into the theatre whenever a new blockbuster film opened. But like James, the theatre has moved on, as well as the pool, the skate park and the DVD store. Now this small town is nothing more than a dustbowl full of old memories.

*

'Come on Michael,' yelled Dad, 'I need your help getting the cattle in the shed.' I sighed to myself. More work to be done. It's one of those days when I wish something more exciting was happening. I scuffed my boots as I walked over to Dad. He was trying to guide an enormous herd of cows out of an old, small tinny gate. I started to help him, slapping the cows' behinds while whistling directions to the dogs.

Everything was going smoothly, like it always does. The large cows were kicking up a large dust cloud, the rhythmic thudding of their feet calming and hypnotic. I felt like sleeping. I started to lie down on my horse's back; it's surprisingly comfortable and I think my horse Barney likes it too. Now I could hear a different noise in the background; a sort of a humming noise. I looked behind me and I could see another large dust cloud.

*

The noise was getting louder and louder; the cloud was getting closer and closer. I looked around at the cows; they were getting really spooked. 'Dad! Dad!' I yelled. I could see he was turning around, trying to see what the commotion was all about. I looked too and now I could make out the silhouette of a large gang of bikies brandishing alcohol bottles. They were getting really close to us now and the herd was freaking out – cows were running around stumbling into each other. The bikies were roaring past us now, hollering and throwing bottles. The cows were now really terrified and some started to bolt. I looked at the bikies; they looked like they might keep riding, but then a couple turned and revved their engines. My heart sank. I tried to warn Dad, but he couldn't hear me over the roar. I knew what they were going to do. The bikers were now riding straight towards the cows. I watched in horror as the whole herd started to bolt away from us.

Christmas Stampede

I looked around in awe as the herd stampeded. The bikies were riding away now. I couldn't understand why they would do this; it just didn't seem right. I looked over at Dad, hoping he would tell me what was going on, but he was chasing after the herd already. I picked up my reins again and joined the chase. My heart was pounding like jungle drums as I rode towards the back of the angry herd and reached the small calves, which were lagging behind. I managed to get them under control, but I was worried that they might run off if I left them there. I really needed to go and help Dad control the herd before we lost them or they hurt themselves. I decided to leave them where they were and tie them together. It took me a couple of minutes to do this. As soon as I'd finished I got back on my horse and galloped off in hot pursuit. Thankfully I could still see the dust cloud; I was gaining on it. I looked around for strays and my eye fell on an old sign, which read 'Vergers Quarry, 13 km'.

As soon as I saw the sign I realised the seriousness of the situation. I had no idea how far away the cows were, so I had to race after them. I hoped Dad had managed to control them, but the lingering dust cloud made me think that maybe he hadn't yet.

I was finally getting closer to the herd. I could almost hear their mournful moaning. As I got closer I saw a couple of cows that had given up and were munching on scarce bits of grass. I looked up, hoping to see the herd, and sure enough I did; but what really caught my attention was the fact that they were getting dangerously close to the quarry cliff face. I was now riding alongside them and I could see Dad at the front, doing his best. When I pulled up next to him, I could see he was sweating profusely. I knew he couldn't do much more; it was my time to shine. I breathed in deep and pulled out in front of the herd.

The adrenalin pumped all around my body. I could feel my heart beating at a hundred k an hour. I needed to act quickly. I headed out further in front of the herd. I realised that there was around one kilometre between me and the cliff and that the herd would probably take a hundred metres to come to a complete stop. This left me with about eight hundred metres to successfully stop them meeting their impending doom. I was really close to the cliff face now; I stopped my horse and slid off, then turned to face the herd. I started to wave my arms around like a madman, screaming at the cows to stop. At first I didn't think it was going to work, but then my horse reared up and let out a loud whinny, and at this they began to stop – slowly, one by one – and were soon walking around as if nothing had happened.

Dad raced over to me yelling with joy. 'Son, you did it! You little beauty, I'm so proud of you boy, so proud! Aha, I think you were right, let's take a break and head into the city to stay with your mum.'

I was so happy now, but not because we were going to the city. I had saved the cows and Dad had said he was proud of me.

*

Years later I still think of this and remember how much fun it was. Dad and I grew closer. I learned to be grateful for what I had. Dad had definitely been right; this was the best Christmas ever.

Christmas Stampede

Mallee Trees and Red Dust

Research and Discussion

1   Where is the narrator from? What do her parents do for a living? Why does her dad need her to help him at the start? Does this same problem also exist in the suburbs, or is it only a problem in the outback? How is Teagan's father tackling this issue and what is he changing now? Is he able to solve the problem at the end of the story? How? Explain with examples from the story.

2   What are Teagan and her family doing when they see the two men with the fox? How does her dad react to this situation? Would he react in the same way if they came across the same men in their backyard in the city? Why? Why does Teagan think her mum does not take her driving?

3   Do you think the relationship between the parents and the teenagers would be different living in the outback from living in the city? How? Give examples from the story as well as your own life to support your views.

Writing and Creating

1   Work with a partner to design a brochure for the town of Nungarin in Western Australia in order to sell the town to tourists in Australia as well as overseas. In your brochure include information on accommodation, tourist attractions, things to do, history, culture, and finally local cuisine and the hospitality of the people.

2   Prepare and conduct a 3–4-minute class debate on whether 'life in the country is better than life in the city'. Have at least three arguments for each side and rebut each other's arguments. Choose an adjudicator and a timekeeper. Use examples in the story as evidence to support your arguments, as well as doing other research online.

3   Find the following words in the story, state which part of speech they belong to and use each of them in a sentence.

a	retaliate	c	profanities	e	scratchily
b	burly	d	monotonous		

Room to Grow

Research and Discussion

1   Where did the main character and her family migrate from? Is the new place a lot different from their old home town? In what ways? What was the narrator's impression when she first arrived in Perth? What was annoying her? Do many people migrate from England to Australia each year? Research and find statistical information on the annual migrant intake from England as well as the reasons for this migration. What is the difference between migrants and refugees or asylum-seekers?

2   What are some of the things Charlie has to do at their new home that she did not do back at their old home? Does she enjoy doing these? Provide examples from the story to support your answer. What are the things she misses from home? Make a list. Discuss with another person at least three things you would miss from your home town if you were to move to a new country, and why you would miss them.

3   Compare Charlie's views about her new home at the start to her feelings and views about it at the end. How are these different? At the end, does she love her new home more than the old one? Give examples of the things she thinks are better in her new farm.

Writing and Creating

1   Find and list the Australian slang words used in the story and write a synonym for each as it would be spoken in England. Write down any other Australian slang terms you know. Find at least six additional words or phrases that are used differently in UK English and US English, for example, caravan (UK) and trailer (US).

2   Imagine you are Riley in the story 'Room to Grow'. Write a letter to one of your friends in England telling them about your new home in Australia. In your letter describe how your views and feelings about the place and the people have changed over time. Talk about your future plans as well and ask your friend about the life you left back in England.

3   You live in the outback and your parents are engineers who work for a private mining company. The company is sending your parents to work in the Middle East for four years. You all need to move there in a week. Write a short story of your family's temporary migration to the Middle East, including your arrival and your first impressions, as well as how these change later on for you and your family. Provide detailed examples of the things you do, the school and the places you go to as well as the culture and the cuisine.

Saying Cheers

Research and Discussion

1   What are the main character and her family celebrating? Research what historic event happened in Australia on 26 January. What is it that Australians celebrate each year on this date? Do you think all Australians are happy to mark this date as a celebration? Why/why not?

2   Where is the protagonist from? How are the protagonist and her family in the story 'Saying Cheers' planning to celebrate Australia Day? How do you and your family celebrate Australia Day?

3   Describe the evening activities enjoyed in the 'Australian way' and the general environment at the home of the protagonist. Do the events of the story reflect the identity of most Australians, and how they live or celebrate Australia Day? Why/why not?

Writing and Creating

1   Read all the Australian colloquial terms below, classify them gramatically and identify which ones were used in the story 'Saying Cheers' and which ones were not used.

a	shoos	e	billabong	i	cheerio
b	snags	f	barbie	j	boomers
c	roos	g	fella	k	ankle-biter
d	ripper	h	jarmies	l	chook

2   With a partner, design a poster portraying the identity of an outback-Aussie family or a bushranger. On your poster include information about Aussie lingo, family life, food, celebrations, daily routine and characteristics in general.

3   Strong and passionate love for one's country can be easily felt and heard in this story by Jaimee Rich. Write the 500–600-word script for a speech you are asked to give as the school captain about what Anzac Day means to teenagers today in Australia. In your speech, first provide the background information of the history of Anzac Day before you talk about why you love Australia and how days such as this and Australia Day are important to the identity of young people and the future of Australia.

Christmas Stampede

Research and Discussion

1   How does Michael usually spend Christmas time on the farm? What does he do that is different from what you do during Christmas? Is he happy to be with his dad during Christmas? Why does he hate summers? What do you do at Christmas and New Year that is usually the same every year? What would you rather do instead one year?

2   Who was Michael's friend once and what happened to him? What were some of the things Michael and his friend did? Why do you think Michael does not do these things any more?

3   What does Michael's father ask Michael to help him with? What happens while Michael and his father are herding the cattle? In what way does Michael manage to help his father that differs from what he does any other time? What is the lesson that Michael learns from this incident? Provide evidence from the story to support your ideas.

Writing and Creating

1   Recreate and write a teenager's manual on either how to herd cattle step-by-step or how to live and be happy in the outback as a teenager, as Michael eventually does in the story 'Christmas Stampede'. Use the second person voice to instruct your readers in your guide.

2   Adverbs are words or phrases that mostly answer the question 'How?' They do this by modifying or qualifying an adjective, verb or other adverb while expressing a relation of place, time, circumstance, manner, cause, degree, etc. For example, *kindly*, *loudly*, *later* and *there* are all adverbs. Find the adverbs used in the story and use them in a paragraph in which you describe life in the outback.

3   Write a journal entry written by Michael on the night of the stampede. Talk in detail about how what started off as a usual day or a usual Christmas turned into a most exciting day for Michael.

Appendix

Alexander Sirian Be

Alexander currently attends a school in Melbourne, Victoria. His family moved to Australia to seek refuge from the Khmer Rouge, and he draws upon these influences to serve as inspiration for his writing. He wishes to continually better himself and grow as a person, to create the tools necessary to bring about a better change in society. His goal is to study commerce at an American university.

Amie Rovacsek

Amie currently attends a school in Perth, Western Australia, and is in year 9. She has a flair for drawing and enjoys all things artistic. She aspires to one day become a veterinarian.

Arun Patel

Arun is a year 7 student at a school in Melbourne. His interests include gaming, watching a bit of television when he gets the chance and the usual things teenagers find interesting. Arun also enjoys reading fiction and although he is unsure whether to become a writer in the future, he enjoys writing creative pieces while he finds his voice.

Ben Black

Ben was born on 22 December 1997 and now lives with his two brothers and parents. He attends a school in Perth, where he is in year 10 this year, and is a part of the Academic Excellence Program at the school.

Catriona Cowie

Catriona is a British student who moved to Australia when she was 10 years old. She enjoys reading and writing short stories and poetry on her online blog. Like her favourite authors, she hopes to capture 'dirty realism' in her writing.

Charlotte Brew

Charlotte is a student at a school in Bathurst, New South Wales. She is 16 years old and is about to enter year 11. Her passions include art, music, reading, writing and science. She hopes to become a trauma surgeon in the Australian Defence Force when she graduates.

Christine Eid

Christine is currently a year 11 student at a school in Melbourne. She is 16 years old and has lived in Melbourne her entire life. She enjoys reading, studying science and art, and writing in any form. She has ambitions to become a wondrous architect to fulfil her passion in creativity and practicality. She hopes to bring change to her little part of the world.

Elena Ng

Elena was born in Australia and is currently 18 years old. In 2012, she graduated as a year 12 student from her high school in Dandenong, Victoria, with plans to study commerce at university. She loves to read, and constantly draws her inspiration to write from her strange dreams.

Elizabeth Morgan

Elizabeth is an eighth-generation Australian and third-generation Darwinite. She has travelled extensively throughout Australia with her parents and seven siblings and especially loves the bush and Australia's unique landscape and history. She has a passion for literature and language, and speaks three different languages, including English. Her other loves include animals and anything out-doorsy.

Erin Caulley

Erin, known by her friends as 'Google', is currently in year 12 at a school in Rockhampton, Queensland. Erin is the Prefect for the History Committee. Her passions include writing, public speaking and history. In the future she hopes to study law, psychology and criminology, and become a lawyer in the criminal system.

Fiona Lam

Fiona attended a school in Sydney, New South Wales, where she completed year 12 in 2012. She plans to study commerce at university and study abroad in New York. Her influences include Haruki Murakami, Ryu Murakami and Ezra Miller.

Helen Qin

Helen was born and raised in Melbourne with a Chinese background. She is currently 17 and a year 11 student at a school in Springvale, Victoria. She enjoys the feel of pen on paper or a blank screen coming to life with one's imagination, as well as public speaking. Her passion is dancing and she trains in ballroom and Latin. She dreams of becoming a media personality and a vet.

Hugh Offor

Hugh is currently a student at a school in Melbourne and grew up in country Victoria. He is 13 and has aspired for several years to become an acclaimed author. He is being mentored by a school English teacher, William Lyon, to assist in this. He has written several fantasy short stories to express his love of imagination.

Jaimee Rich

Jaimee lives in the hills area of Perth. She is currently 15 years of age and in year 10 at a school in Perth. Her passions are playing basketball and riding horses. One day she hopes to have a career in medicine, criminology or vet science, and to become a professional basketball player.

Jasmine Yiamkiati

Jasmine is 16 years old and comes from a Filipino and Thai background. She attends a school in Parramatta, New South Wales, and has a passion for reading, writing and travel. She would love to see the whole world and, when she is older, hopes to be able to work with animals or in the literary industry.

Jessica Chisholm

Jessica is a seventh-generation Australian and is currently attending a school in the Perth Hills. She is 14 years old and has a passion for writing and literature, along with music and environmental science. After high school, Jessica wishes to study biochemistry and molecular biology at university.

Karen Huang

Karen was born in Australia and completed high school in 2012. She spent most of her childhood in China with her uncle and aunt. Seventy per cent of her makes no sense, 30 per cent is normal and 0.0000001 per cent is her literary genius. Her hobby is film making. Her goal is to study medicine and become a cardiologist. Her dream is to become a reliable pillar of her family.

Karyn Tee

Karyn is 17 and finished year 12 at a school in Adelaide, South Australia, in 2012. She has lived in Australia all her life but has a strong interest in different cultures as well. She loves the endless possibilities of creating new worlds through writing. Although she still has not decided upon a career to pursue, she hopes to help foster a sense of global community and cultural understanding in whatever she does.

Keeley Roberts

Keeley is currently a student at a school in Kingston, Tasmania. She has spent her whole childhood living in Tasmania and writes about experiences that have happened in her life. She loves music, things that challenge her and writing stories about her own life.

Matthew Hill

Matthew is a student attending a school in Perth. He enjoys going out with friends, and playing sports and games, and hopes to finish school and attend university.

Maya Simpson

Maya was born in England and moved to Australia at the age of eight. She currently attends a school in Perth. As well as writing, she enjoys dance, swimming and acting. She hopes to go to university and study psychology.

Milan Kantor

Milan was born in Australia and attends a school in Melbourne. He is currently in year 10 and hopes to travel to America to attend university. Besides his passion for writing, he also enjoys swimming and acting.

Rose Rosen

Rose was born in Broken Hill, New South Wales, and grew up in the red desert learning that if she was ever stranded without water, she should chew on the saltbush. Having since moved to more urban areas such survival methods haven't been necessary but she still remains a child from the red centre.

Rosie McCrossin

Rosie is 14 years old and attends a school in Brisbane, Queensland. Public transport is where she finds the inspiration for her story characters (she's the one sitting in the corner with the notebook).

Ryan Harris

Ryan was born in the Northern Territory in 1998. He currently attends a school in Perth and enjoys sports and other school activities.

Samantha Go

Samantha is a 15-year-old girl, born in Australia. Her father is Filipino and her mother is an Australian-born Chinese. She is currently in year 9, studying at a school in Dundas, New South Wales. Besides writing, other passions of hers include crafting, drawing and filming.

Shaun Moeller

Shaun currently attends a school in the Perth Hills and is in year 9. In the future he wants to study electrical engineering or sports science.

Teagan Brandis

Teagan attends a school in Perth and is currently in year 9. She moved from a small country town, Nungarin, to Perth when she was four and inherited a flair for poetry and art from her parents.

Printed in the United States
by Baker & Taylor Publisher Services